SEXUAL HARASSMENT AND CULTURAL CHANGE IN WRITING STUDIES

PRACTICES & POSSIBILITIES

Series Editors: Nick Carbone, Mike Palmquist, Aimee McClure, and Aleashia Walton

Series Associate Editor: Karen-Elizabeth Moroski

The Practices & Possibilities Series addresses the full range of practices within the field of Writing Studies, including teaching, learning, research, and theory. From Joseph Williams' reflections on problems to Richard E. Young's taxonomy of "small genres" to Adam Mackie's considerations of technology, the books in this series explore issues and ideas of interest to writers, teachers, researchers, and theorists who share an interest in improving existing practices and exploring new possibilities. The series includes both original and republished books. Works in the series are organized topically.

The WAC Clearinghouse, Colorado State University Open Press, and University Press of Colorado are collaborating so that these books will be widely available through free digital distribution and low-cost print editions. The publishers and the series editors are committed to the principle that knowledge should freely circulate. We see the opportunities that new technologies have for further democratizing knowledge. And we see that to share the power of writing is to share the means for all to articulate their needs, interest, and learning into the great experiment of literacy.

OTHER BOOKS IN THE SERIES

Ryan J. Dippre, Talk, Tools, and Texts: A Logic-in-Use for Studying Lifespan Literate Action Development (2019)

Jessie Borgman and Casey McArdle, *Personal, Accessible, Responsive, Strategic: Resources and Strategies for Online Writing Instructors* (2019)

Cheryl Geisler & Jason Swarts, Coding *Streams of Language: Techniques for the Systematic Coding of Text, Talk, and Other Verbal Data* (2019)

Ellen C. Carillo, *A Guide to Mindful Reading* (2017)

Lillian Craton, Renée Love & Sean Barnette (Eds.), *Writing Pathways to Student Success* (2017)

Charles Bazerman, *Involved: Writing for College, Writing for Your Self* (2015)

Adam Mackie, *New Literacies Dictionary: Primer for the Twenty-first Century Learner* (2011)

Patricia A. Dunn, *Learning Re-abled: The Learning Disability Controversy and Composition Studies* (2011)

Richard E. Young, *Toward A Taxonomy of "Small" Genres and Writing Techniques for Writing Across the Curriculum* (2011)

Joseph M. Williams, *Problems into PROBLEMS: A Rhetoric of Motivation* (2011)

SEXUAL HARASSMENT AND CULTURAL CHANGE IN WRITING STUDIES

Edited by Patricia Freitag Ericsson

The WAC Clearinghouse
wac.colostate.edu
Fort Collins, Colorado

University Press of Colorado
upcolorado.com
Louisville, Colorado

The WAC Clearinghouse, Fort Collins, Colorado 80523

University Press of Colorado, Louisville, Colorado 80027

ISBN 978-1-64215-098-8 (PDF) | 978-1-64215-099-5 (ePub) | 978-1-64642-104-6 (pbk.)

DOI 10.37514/PRA-B.2020.0988

Printed in the United States of America

Library of Congress Cataloging-in-Publication Data

Names: Ericsson, Patricia Freitag, 1950– editor.
Title: Sexual harassment and cultural change in writing studies / edited by Patricia Freitag Ericsson.
Description: Fort Collins, Colorado : WAC Clearinghouse, [2020] | Series: Practices & possibilities | Includes bibliographical references.
Identifiers: LCCN 2020017316 (print) | LCCN 2020017317 (ebook) | ISBN 9781646421046 (paperback) | ISBN 9781642150988 (pdf) | ISBN 9781642150995 (epub)
Subjects: LCSH: Sexual harassment. | Sexual harassment—Prevention. | Sexual harassment—Study and teaching.
Classification: LCC HD6060.3 .S48 2020 (print) | LCC HD6060.3 (ebook) | DDC 808.0071/1—dc23
LC record available at https://lccn.loc.gov/2020017316
LC ebook record available at https://lccn.loc.gov/2020017317

Copyeditor: Aimee McClure
Designer: Mike Palmquist
Cover Image: Pickrep.com (https://www.pikrepo.com/ftdzm/assorted-jigsaw-puzzle-piece-lot)
Series Editors: Nick Carbone, Mike Palmquist, Aimee McClure, and Aleashia Walton
Series Associate Editor: Karen-Elizabeth Moroski

The WAC Clearinghouse supports teachers of writing across the disciplines. Hosted by Colorado State University, and supported by the Colorado State University Open Press, it brings together scholarly journals and book series as well as resources for teachers who use writing in their courses. This book is available in digital formats for free download at wac.colostate.edu.

Founded in 1965, the University Press of Colorado is a nonprofit cooperative publishing enterprise supported, in part, by Adams State University, Colorado State University, Fort Lewis College, Metropolitan State University of Denver, University of Colorado, University of Northern Colorado, University of Wyoming, Utah State University, and Western Colorado University. For more information, visit upcolorado.com.

Contents

Acknowledgments

As editor of this collection, I write with deep appreciation for the dozens of people who made it possible. Those include the participants of the WPA-L listserv who contributed to online discussions that were the genesis of this text; those who responded to the quest to do something positive in response to that listerv discussion; those who signed on to brainstorm ideas and sort through the messiness of what it might be; those who were willing to dig in and get their hands dirty in writing, researching, organizing, and wrestling with this difficult topic; those who had flashbacks and nightmares because of their willingness to engage; those who came on board later in the game when efforts were flagging; all of these, and more. I am especially thankful for those whose work appears in these pages: Aaron Barlow, Darsie Bowden, Kefaya Diab, William Duffy, Ti Macklin, Craig A. Meyer, Whitney Myers, Mark Shealy, Diana Winslow, and Kathleen Blake Yancey. Without them, this collection would not exist.

Throughout the process, this book has been steadfastly supported by the series editors. Mike Palmquist's initial response to the project was whole-heartedly positive, and his commitment to it has never diminished. The support of the other members of the editorial team, Nick Carbone and Aimee McClure, has been flawless. My thanks would not be complete without acknowledging Katie McWain whose conversation, commentary, and enthusiastic support helped keep this project afloat. As our editorial assistant for over a year, Katie had a hand in every chapter, but I am particularly grateful for her help in making Chapter 3 significantly better. After reading a draft of that chapter and offering detailed advice, Katie wrote, "This is such an important project that I'm excited to continue reading as it develops!" Sadly and tragically, Katie left us as the book was nearing completion. I don't know if she ever had a chance to read Chapter 3 again, but if she did, she would have seen her fingerprints all over it.

Our reviewers were diligent, incisive, and kind in their insights and suggestions on how to make the book stronger. Toward the end of the project, I leaned heavily on a few contributors for additional editorial help. And I also engaged trusted readers, Anna Plemons and Simone Droge, who provided fresh-eyed insights. Throughout the process, Preston Andrews has been a sounding board whose wise and loving counsel has (as always) kept me composed and focused.

I never imagined that a book on this topic might be my final contribution to the discipline I have worked in for over 35 years. I wish it wasn't. I wish this issue had been solved long ago. But I know too well it is a sickness that still infects our culture. I spent an hour tonight talking with my 19-year-old granddaughter who is living through, crying through this very issue in 2020. I couldn't solve her situation, but her tearful refrain "I shouldn't have to be dealing with this!" echoed my thinking and my wish—this issue should have been solved long ago. This book needs to be published. Action needs to be taken. Our job is to make trouble for those who carry and spread this toxic disease.

SEXUAL HARASSMENT AND CULTURAL CHANGE IN WRITING STUDIES

Introduction

Patricia Freitag Ericsson
WASHINGTON STATE UNIVERSITY

The genesis of this book was a listserv discussion related to the burgeoning harassment news stories of 2017. Eleven days before *The Atlantic* asked, "When Will the 'Harvey Effect' Reach Academia?" (Fredrickson, 2017) a woman using the pseudonym, "Melissa Hitchenson," and the subject line, "We have Weinstein problem," confronted the issue on the WPA-L Listserv[1] (October 19, 2017):

> I'm writing to you all because I want the field to face up to the fact that we are not exempt from having a problem with misogyny and sexual harassment in the field, often by powerful men in positions of authority in writing programs. I share my experience, under a pseudonym, with the hopes that this field that prides itself on its "niceness" can stare this issue in the face rather than ignore it. (WPA archives)

"Melissa" went on to detail her own experiences, writing, "I stayed quiet then, but I can't stay quiet any longer." She ended her post with the hallmark hashtag of the movement: #metoo. Posts to that discussion thread ranged from informative to confessional to wary. Included were #metoo stories, controversies about whether or not to name names, references to scholars whose work might be helpful, and more. The angst-filled conversation came from all areas of writing studies: classroom teaching, scholarship, mentorship, research, writing centers, graduate studies, and more.

Although the tone of the thread was generally supportive, precious little of the discussion concerned what we (as listserv participants or as individuals) could do that was proactive. The listserv conversation led to this post by Patricia Ericsson:

> This is my proactive attempt at doing something. If it does even a small bit of good, then it will be somewhat gratifying. I have been searching for this kind of case study and have found a few. Most, however, are not in the academic world. Those outside have some application, but I'd like some that are more oriented to the kinds of situations we [in writing studies] face in aca-

---

1. WPA-L is an international e-mail discussion list intended primarily for individuals who are involved in writing program administration at universities, colleges, or community colleges. WPA-L's publicly searchable archives (https://lists.asu.edu/cgi-bin/wa?Ao=wpa-l) provide access to the entire conversation.

DOI: https://doi.org/10.37514/PRA-B.2020.0988.1.3

3

deme. My hope is to archive a curated collection of these case studies and make them available to all.

A possible process: 1) If you know of a collection like this, let us all know. Perhaps we don't need this if a collection already exists. 2) Volunteer to help put this together. Most case study collections have a somewhat uniform format. We'd work on that. You can contact me on the listserv or at my email if you'd rather do it back channel. 3) ???? your suggestions.

Within 20 minutes there was one positive reply; within a few days, a dozen people expressed interest in building writing studies resources regarding sexual harassment. Those responses and further conversations led to this book.

Chapter 1 details some of the previous scholarship on this topic, both inside and outside the academy, but readers will not be surprised that sexual harassment is not a new issue. With the women's movement in the 1970s, however, open discussions of gender relationships in the workplace became more widespread in the US. The term "sexual harassment" appears to have come into the lexicon in the mid–1970's. In a 2017 opinion piece, Lin Farley claims to have coined the term stating, "It wasn't until April 1975 that women had a word for talking about what their male bosses were doing to them. It was that month that I first used the phrase "sexual harassment" in public, during a hearing on women in the workplace by the New York City Human Rights Commission, at which I was testifying as an instructor at Cornell University" (Farley, 2017, para. 2). A 1975 *New York Times* account of research done by Farley and the Cornell Human Affairs Program found that 70% of the 155 female respondents had experienced sexual harassment (Nemy, para. 7). Reading the anecdotes that resulted from this study belie the 1970s Virginia Slims "You've Come a Long Way Baby" advertising campaign. Sadly, the same ad campaign would still be inaccurate today.

One of the questions the authors of this book initially asked was "Should there be a separate book about sexual harassment for writing studies?[2] Despite there being considerable scholarly attention to sexual harassment in the academy, writing studies includes pedagogical approaches and unique relationships that make the discipline more open to concerns of sexual harassment. If not carefully considered, pedagogical approaches in writing studies can provide for social interactions that could lead to possibly questionable interactions. Whether in tutoring, one-on-one student conferencing, graduate student mentoring, or classrooms, writing studies' highly valued social, community approaches can open the door to harassment. Although he complicates the idea of community, Joseph Harris (2012) provided an insightful gloss of writing studies' approach to

---

2. This book takes a broad approach to writing studies, understanding it as including composition, rhetoric, writing centers, writing program administration, independent writing studies programs and those housed in English departments, and more.

community, "We write not as isolated individuals but as members of communities whose beliefs, concerns, and practices both instigate and constrain, at least in part, the sorts of things we can say" (pp. 133–134). Inviting undergraduates, graduate students, and colleagues into a "community," Harris posits, bids participants to become part of a community of power (p. 135). These communities of power are, however, communities of unequal power, rife with harassment possibilities. Whether these power communities are located in tutoring sessions, student conferences, small classes, or mentoring experiences, the power structure is not balanced, even though some of our most vaunted pedagogical ideals purport it to be.

Best practices in writing studies frequently include invitations to write and talk about challenging topics. Even when our writing assignments and research topics are seemingly not personal, threads of the personal often underlie them. In fact, many assignments and research projects start with personal connections. Challenging topics provide for lively conversations in undergraduate classrooms, graduate seminars, and even hallway conversations. Ideas, even disclosures, from these conversations can leak into day-to-day associations. Complex relationships can develop, and these relationships may include sensitive, personal topics. The writing that grows from writing studies scholarship and pedagogy is often central in one-on-one interactions at open tables in writing centers or over a desk in a private office. The personal is invited, but such invitations can create situations in which a sense of trust can be taken advantage of or betrayed. These betrayals are too often a surprise to those who have trusted the invitation to community, not aware that the community is one saturated in power relationships.

Although Chapter 4 provides more on the issue of power relationships, it is vital to know that virtually all the published articles and books on sexual harassment point to power (sometimes coded as "status") as a core consideration. In the 1990 book, *Ivory Power: Sexual Harassment on Campus*, Vita C. Rabinowitz stated the power that professors have might be "indirect" and thus "more subtly exercised," but then went on to claim that "In fact, professors wield a great deal of power over students who depend on them for grades, letters of recommendation, academic and career counseling, and research and clinical opportunities" (p. 104). Higher education is saturated with power relationships that can impact individuals at all levels whether undergraduates, graduate students, staff, or faculty. Because of our pedagogy, small class sizes, and frequent one-on-one encounters, writing studies is super-saturated with power relationships.

Foremost in the minds of those who have contributed to this book is the commitment to making it a learning resource. It is not an in-depth study of the social, psychological, or even the rhetorical roots of sexual harassment. It is not a trove of legal knowledge on the topic. It is not a step-by-step guide to an undoing of all the societal and personal wrongs that will lead to a world unscathed by sexual harassment (although if we could write such a book, we would!). Instead of being daunted and demoralized by what it is not, those of us who contributed to this book have played to our strengths. This book is a resource that provides the groundwork for understanding sexual harassment as well as encouraging the often-difficult conversations that are steps to awareness, action, and prevention of it. Perhaps most importantly, this text mandates a heightened consciousness of sexual harassment as a cultural issue and underscores the profound commitment to cultural change that is necessary to eradicate sexual harassment. This book is about driving the conversation toward increased awareness of sexual harassment as a cultural issue while providing a meaningful resource from which to learn how substantive action might be taken.

As the book was taking shape, the authors thoughtfully considered the venues in which it might be useful. Our approach encompassed composition, rhetoric, writing centers, and writing program administration, but we envisioned the book being used beyond the discipline in campus committees that focus on curriculum, general education, and diversity, equity, and inclusion. It can be a resource for new-faculty development or training faculty for leadership positions. For those leading programs (writing program administrators, directors of composition, writing center directors, writing across the curriculum program directors, and more) it can be a dynamic resource easily adaptable for workshops and classes. For those preparing peer tutors, the book can provide guidance in the interpersonal dynamics at work in student sessions. It can be a foundational text in any pedagogy class—at either the graduate or undergraduate level. As a resource and handbook, it can be used to support graduate students moving into leadership positions. In disciplines outside of writing studies, the book can be used as a kind of template for best-practice approaches in preventing sexual harassment. Those disciplines could write their own, discipline-specific scenarios, but use other parts of the book as appropriate. We see the book being used to start conversations, construct training, and improve policy—all of these in the contexts of local situations and constraints.

In organizing this book, the authors were mindful of the need for a deeper and more nuanced understanding of sexual harassment. A reader could jump directly into Chapter 4 and start opining on the scenarios. This short-cut is tempting, and some will, no doubt, take it. But a productive dialogue about those scenarios requires historical context, definitional clarity, and knowledge of policies that govern institutional responses.

Chapter 1: "Digging In" provides a brief background on sexual harassment, moving from its history in the general public, to the academic world, and then narrowing to writing studies. All of this background is important, but perhaps none of it more important than elucidating the need for this book in writing studies. Despite this field's concern about a variety of social issues, a similar concern about sexual harassment has been sorely missing. In Chapter 2: "Defining It" the reader will find eleven terms approached through definitions in the popular press, legal research, and, perhaps most importantly, higher education. Admittedly defining terms is not the cure-all for addressing sexual harassment, but definitions are a necessary foundation for tackling the issue. Chapter 3: "Baking

It In" provides several approaches to enacting the cultural change needed to fight against sexual harassment. These approaches were chosen because significant research has gone into evaluating their effectiveness. In addition, they are suitable for academic institutions and the particular challenges of writing studies. Chapter 4: "Talking About It" provides an in-depth opportunity to apply the ideas from the first three chapters. All scenarios are fictional, but they will sound familiar to far too many readers. Simple, uncomplicated analyses of the scenarios are not provided because that would close off the opportunity for thinking, discussion, and multifaceted considerations of them. Readers are encouraged to use the definitional grounding provided by Chapter 2, the proactive approaches detailed in Chapter 3, the Discussion Questions that follow each scenario, as well as variety of critical lenses to analyze the scenarios. Closing the book, Chapter 5: "Learning More About It" is an extensive bibliography for those who want to pursue further study.

Considerable thought was given to including an additional chapter that would tie things up neatly, provide a recipe for success, or offer a step-by-step guide to eliminating sexual harassment. But that kind of chapter would belie the complexity of the cultural change needed to combat sexual harassment. It would also ignore the reality that such change is local, focused on relationships, and requires leadership that is adaptable and flexible (Maimon, 2018, p. 5). Realizing that a neat concluding chapter might uncomplicate what we know is a complicated, thorny, and intractable issue, that chapter was not written. In reality, it might have been an impossible chapter to write.

Chapter 1: Digging In

Ti Macklin
BOISE STATE UNIVERSITY

Craig A. Meyer
TEXAS A&M UNIVERSITY KINGSVILLE

Patricia Freitag Ericsson
WASHINGTON STATE UNIVERSITY

Sexual harassment is embedded in our government, schools, entertainment, and our culture. But the term "sexual harassment" is relatively new, coming into the lexicon in the 1970s. The U.S. Equal Employment Opportunity Commission (EEOC) defines sexual harassment as:

> Unwelcome sexual advances, requests for sexual favors, and other verbal or physical conduct of a sexual nature constitute sexual harassment when this conduct explicitly or implicitly affects an individual's employment, unreasonably interferes with an individual's work performance, or creates an intimidating, hostile, or offensive work environment. ("Facts" n.d., para. 2)

While this definition is widely recognized, employers and institutions often have more detailed and fine-grained variations. Chapter 2: "Defining It" provides definitions of sexual harassment from a wide range of sources, allowing readers to consider the ways in which institutional culture may impact considerations of sexual harassment even at the definitional level.

Part of the difficulty in defining sexual harassment, however, stems from an inclination to view harassment solely as a legal issue. In her 2007 book, Carrie N. Baker argued that the movement against sexual harassment started with the goal of systemic cultural shifts, but soon became an individual and legal endeavor (p. 6). Viewing sexual harassment as an individual, legal issue is part of the problem with recognition and elimination of sexual harassment. A legalistic, limited understanding distances sexual harassment from broader cultural life.

Another result of the focus on the individual is the tendency to blame the victim. In fact, the EEOC's "Facts about Sexual Harassment" web page suggests that victims of sexual harassment should "inform the harasser directly that the conduct is unwelcome and must stop" (n.d., para. 4). In other words, the EEOC suggests the initial confrontation about sexual harassment should be by the victim to the abuser. One of the challenges this book takes on is that of understanding that sexual harassment is a cultural issue, not an individual, legal one.

DOI: https://doi.org/10.37514/PRA-B.2020.0988.2.01

Sexual harassment has made news for decades, but it has not typically been a front-page issue. It became a headline issue in 1991 with *The New York Times* (Section A Page 1) article entitled "Law Professor Accuses Thomas of Sexual Harassment in the 1980s" (Lewis). One day after this headline, Maureen Dowd commented on the dynamics of the Judiciary Committee writing ". . . the story of how members of the all-male Judiciary Committee handled the allegations has touched off an angry explosion among women in legal and political circles" (1991, para. 2). These hearings brought sexual harassment into the light of day, but the impact of the "angry explosion" that Dowd mentioned reached a small audience. In a 2019 interview, Anita Hill recalled "after the hearings, 70 percent— or at least a pretty wide majority of people—thought that I had perjured myself. Most of the people polled, regardless of race, regardless of gender, believed that Clarence Thomas should be confirmed for the Supreme Court" (Bennett, 2019, para. 5). "Many people viewing the hearings," she continued, "didn't even realize that sexual harassment was something that was actionable, that they could file a complaint about. They had no idea what the concept was about." Since 1991, Hill believes things have changed gradually "because people started telling their stories, we started filing complaints, we had lawsuits that were filed, and the public became much more aware" (para. 6).

Almost 30 years after it first made headlines, sexual harassment once again became Section A, Page 1 news with *The New York Times* expose on Harvey Weinstein (Kantor and Twohey, 2019). Beginning with that article, the breadth and depth of Weinstein's purported crimes have been thoroughly chronicled ("Harvey Weinstein," 2019). As Hollywood news intensified, encompassing more and more actors, directors, and others in that community, awareness of sexual harassment in other populations escalated.

The academic community began adding its stories to the tsunami of reports with Karen Kelsky's 2017 blog-based, crowd-sourced survey becoming one of the most active venues for reporting. Created on November 30, Kelsky's survey generated 1,567 responses in about ten days (Ellis, para. 3). As of August 2018 (when submissions closed), the blog's spreadsheet included 2438 entries (Kelsky). The *Chronicle of Higher Education*'s 2017 article on revelations of sexual harassment in higher education since the Weinstein expose is equally overwhelming as it provides a running guide of high-profile reports made for over a year (Gluckman, Read, Mangan & Quilantan, 2017). Anyone paying attention to the news on reported incidences of sexual harassment in academia has seen a cascade of cases making the news since 2017.

From the predatory professor who targets first-year students to the all-too-familiar powerful administrator who fails to address reported incidents, sexual harassment is nearly a commonplace in the academic world. Although action against sexual harassment became possible in the 1960s when Title VII of the 1964 Civil Rights Act established sexual discrimination in employment as illegal, it was not until 1980 that the Equal Employment Opportunity Commission provided guidelines on sexual harassment ("Notice," 1990, Section 4, para. 3). In the intervening years, a Yale student brought one of the first widely publicized cases of sexual harassment to the courts in 1977 (Henry, 1977). Despite the *Alexander vs. Yale University* case being decided in favor of Yale, many scholars have noted that the 1980 case led many universities to institute their first policies on sexual harassment.

Although the Conference on College Composition and Communication issued the "CCCC Standards for Ethical Conduct Regarding Sexual Violence, Sexual Harassment, and Hostile Environments" in 2016, there remains surprisingly little scholarship that specifically addresses sexual harassment in writing studies' books and journals both prior to and since the "Standards'" publication. Writing studies scholarship has examined all manner of advocacy and activism, with little explicit discussion of sexual harassment.

Those familiar with writing studies research know the field is typically unafraid to tackle sweeping social issues. A quick search of activist scholarship in writing studies finds scholarship on the political economies of composition (Scott, 2009; Welch & Scott, 2016); labor issues (Horning, 2016; Kahn, Lalicker & Lynch-Biniek, 2017; Penrose, 2012; Schell & Stock, 2001); and racism (Condon & Young, 2013; Inoue, 2015, 2019; Inoue & Poe, 2012; Lamos, 2018; Perryman-Clark, 2016; Poe, Inoue & Elliot, 2018; Villanueva, 2006). A good deal of activist scholarship also focuses on inclusivity and discrimination by language use (Cushman, 2016; Horner, Lu, Royster & Trimbur, 2011), sex, gender, and sexual orientation (Alexander & Rhodes, 2011; Daniel, 2006; Geiger, 2013; Royster, 2000), and ability (Dolmage, 2017; Garrett, 2018; Wood, Dolmage, Price & Lewiecki-Wilson, 2014) as they pertain to language, writing, and rhetoric. This representative sample of writing studies scholarship indicates a strong commitment to advocacy and illustrates a substantial record of advocating for a broad range of social issues—with the notable exception of sexual harassment.

Before 2017, writing studies scholarship concerning sexual harassment was rare. Some examples include Jeffrey Carroll's (1992) "Freshmen: Confronting Sexual Harassment in the Classroom," Julia Ferganchick-Neufang's (1997) "Harassment On-Line," Tony Filipovitch and Mary McDearmon's (1998) "The Case of the Harassed Teacher" and Margaret Weaver's 2004 "Censoring What Tutors' Clothing Says: First Amendment Rights/Writes within Tutorial Space."

Since 2017, more concern about issues of sexual harassment has begun to appear in English Studies publications. In 2018, Tara Star Johnson and Shea Kerkhoff's editorial in *English Education* examined sexual harassment from a disciplinary perspective and stated their hope that "The field of English education can be part of the paradigm shift, a move to a culture of consent. A culture that moves the onus to stop sexual assault from victims to perpetrators" (p. 14). Also in 2018, *Composition Studies Journal* published six short vignettes on sexual harassment in the *Journal's* "Where we are" section which highlights current and compelling issues. Included in this particular section, "#Metoo and Academia," were a variety of pieces from graduate students and faculty that highlighted the breadth of the problem and suggested ideas for solving it. Laura R. Micciche, the editor of *Composition Studies*, categorized the pieces as "infuriating and depressing," but noted, "we need them." Micciche's "hope is that the stories included in this issue spark a wider sustained conversation including more voices, led by those who occupy (relative) positions of power, and motivate accountability measures that ensure the safety of students and teachers alike" (p. 11). In addition to accountability, in a 2019 *Composition Forum* article T Passwater elucidated a "safe space pedagogy" imagined as a "building project, not a fixed pedagogy: to build an infrastructure of different pathways for different bodies (para. 57). This kind of writing studies pedagogy disrupts power structures, a disruption necessary to bring about cultural change.

The commitment to activism, social justice, and inclusivity regularly encouraged in writing studies demands a more serious, in-depth looks at sexual harassment. Even though the Conference on College Composition and Communication has an entire web page devoted to "Advocacy and Activism," that page makes no mention of preventing sexual harassment as a necessary form of activism. As a discipline of inclusivity, writing studies must directly address sexual harassment in classrooms, workplaces, and institutions. This book furthers that goal, encouraging research and discussions that will help writing studies professionals to take meaningful action to "dig in" and work to "bake in" the cultural changes needed.

Chapter 2: Defining It—
Terms and Definitions

Craig A. Meyer
TEXAS A&M UNIVERSITY KINGSVILLE

Kefaya Diab
INDIANA UNIVERSITY

Mark Shealy
TENNESSEE TECH UNIVERSITY

Aaron Barlow
NEW YORK CITY COLLEGE OF TECHNOLOGY

Patricia Freitag Ericsson
WASHINGTON STATE UNIVERSITY

One of the most thought-provoking challenges in sexual harassment discussions is defining terms. This chapter invites readers to consider a variety of definitions and subcategories before jumping into other chapters, especially Chapter 4 in which readers are invited to interrogate sexual harassment scenarios. Admittedly, there are pitfalls in leaning too heavily on definitions. Following the unattributed adage "To define the terms is to win the argument" to its extreme may result in reducing dialogue about sexual harassment to a narrow, unproductive contest. Despite this drawback, the definition of terms is fundamental to this project.

The importance of definitions was emphasized in Mark V. Roehling and Jason Huang's 2018 article in which they argued that misalignment and confusion about definitions can cause problems in sexual harassment training and make the results of such training difficult to ascertain. This is especially important, they assert, when scenario-based training asks participants to make judgments about particular situations (p. 135–136). This chapter, however, takes into account the fact that definitions are rhetorical constructions in which choice of words, hierarchy of presentation, subtleties of punctuation, and more can make for substantive differences. Because writing studies professionals know the importance of such differences, this chapter invites readers to dig into a variety of definitions to gain a deeper and more nuanced understanding of sexual harassment. Even though this rhetorical approach may not result in the precise definitions Roehling and Huang would prefer, considering nuances allows readers to take into account the contexts, both local and cultural, in which the definitions were created and the differences those contexts make. Definitions alone cannot make the kind of cultural

DOI: https://doi.org/10.37514/PRA-B.2020.0988.2.02

change needed to curb sexual harassment, but considering them can provide the foundation necessary for the conversations that can lead to cultural change.

Understanding that sexual harassment is a type of sexual discrimination is an important step in definitions. Sexual discrimination is a broad term that includes many types of behavior. According to the Equal Employment Opportunity Commission, "Sex discrimination involves treating someone (an applicant or employee) unfavorably because of that person's sex" ("Sex-based discrimination," n.d. para. 1). The foundation of this kind of discrimination is unequal treatment on the basis of sex, including hiring practices, pay, office space, and more. Sexual harassment, a substantial category of sexual discrimination, is typically broken down into several sub-categories. This chapter defines sexual harassment as well as ten sub-categories that the contributors deemed important.

Each definition follows a general pattern: first, popular press, followed by legal, and then institutional definitions. The ten sub-categories (in alphabetic order):

- Bullying
- Gender
- Hostile Work Environment
- Mandatory Reporting
- Microaggression
- Quid pro quo
- Rape
- Retaliation
- Sexual Assault
- Stalking

Two parts of the Civil Rights Act of 1964 (as amended in 1972), Title VII and Title IV, are also included, though without the definitional breakdown applied to the above.

Discussion of the definitions may be supported by the following questions, as well as many more:

- How do definitions from different sources (i.e. from popular press to institutional) converge or diverge?
- Where do institutional definitions originate (URLs may help determine the source)? How might these differences of institutional unit origin influence definitions? How do these institutional definitions position different stakeholders: administrators, faculty, staff, and students?
- Are the definitions provided similar to or different from those of your current institution?

Defining Sexual Harassment

Sexual harassment is employed as an overarching term. It is useful to understand the term and to also realize it demands sub-categories to be constructively applied.

Popular Press Understanding

Sexual harassment includes teasing, sexual advances, and unwelcome touching. It might involve jokes or taunting directed at an individual because of her gender. It can include promises of promotion or pay raises in exchange for sexual favors, although sexual harassment is not limited to interactions with the victim's employer or supervisor.

- https://www.thebalancecareers.com/sex-discrimination-vs-gender-discrimination-3515722

Legal Resource Definition

A unique form of sex discrimination is sexual harassment. Women and men have the right to secure and perform their jobs free of unwanted demands for romantic or sexual relationships, or unwanted communications or behaviors of a sexual nature that interfere with their ability to work.

- https://employment.findlaw.com/employment-discrimination/sex-gender-discrimination-overview.html

Higher Education Definitions

Community College of Rhode Island

Sexual harassment is coerced, unethical and/or unwanted sexual attention which includes verbal harassment and suggestions, rape, and sexual assault. Legally, sexual harassment is viewed in terms of the impact of the behavior, not the intent of the alleged perpetrator. If you have been hassled or touched in any way and you did not consent, this is considered harassment.

- Victims and harassers can be of any age, gender, or orientation, and can be of the same gender.
- If conduct is unwelcome or perceived as harassment, then it IS harassment.

- https://www.ccri.edu/doss/deanstudents/gender_equity/harassment.html

Utah State University

Sexual harassment is unwelcome sexual advances, requests for sexual favors, and other verbal or physical conduct of a sexual nature when:

- Submission to such conduct is made either explicitly or implicitly a term or condition of an individual's employment or status as a student in a course, program or activity.
- Submission to or rejection of such conduct by an individual is used as the basis for employment or academic decisions affecting an individual.

- Such conduct has the purpose or effect of unreasonably interfering with an individual's work or academic performance, or of creating an intimidating, hostile or offensive environment for working or learning

🌐 https://www.usu.edu/sexual-assault/definitions/index

Gonzaga University

Harassment and discrimination against individuals in protected classes can take many forms. It can include verbal or physical conduct, name-calling, slurs, comments, rumors, jokes, innuendos, unwelcome compliments or touching, cartoons, pranks, graphic and written statements, communications via cell phones or the internet, or other conduct which may be physically or emotionally threatening, harmful or humiliating. Generally, physical and verbal conduct is considered harassment when it meets one or more of the following criteria:

- Submission to the undesirable conduct or communication is made, either explicitly or implicitly, a term or condition of one's employment or academic status, or
- Submission to or rejection of the conduct or communication by an individual is used as a factor in decisions affecting the individual's employment or education, or
- The conduct or communication has the purpose or effect of substantially or unreasonably interfering with an individual's employment or education, or creates an intimidating, hostile, or offensive employment or academic environment, and
- The conduct or communication would not have occurred but for the protected category of the individual(s) or group to whom it is directed or who are affected by it.

🌐 https://www.gonzaga.edu/student-life/student-services/resolution-center /student-code-of-conduct/university-standards-of-conduct/harassment-dis crimination-policy

Defining the Ten Subcategories

Bullying

Bullying is not always sexual harassment. In their 2019 edited collection on bullying, Cristyn L. Elder and Bethany Davila maintain that bullying is an "endemic problem" (p. 9), and they go into significant detail to define bullying in different institutional contexts, especially as bullying is related to writing program administrators. They explicitly note that their book does "not address matters of sexual harassment, which is distinct from, though often accompanied by, bullying behaviors" (p. 13). Because of this difference, definitions of bullying are important in considering whether actions are sexual harassment or not.

Popular Press Understanding

Bullying is an intentional behavior that hurts, harms, or humiliates a student, either physically or emotionally, and can happen while at school, in the community, or online. Those bullying often have more social or physical "power," while those targeted have difficulty stopping the behavior. The behavior is typically repeated, though it can be a one-time incident.

🌎 https://www.pacer.org/bullying/resources/info-facts.asp

Legal Resource Definition

Bullying is generally defined as an intentional act that causes harm to others, and may involve verbal harassment, verbal or non-verbal threats, physical assault, stalking, or other methods of coercion such as manipulation, blackmail, or extortion. It is aggressive behavior that intends to hurt, threaten or frighten another person. An imbalance of power between the aggressor and the victim is often involved. Bullying occurs in a variety of contexts, such as schools, workplaces, political or military settings, and others.

🌎 https://definitions.uslegal.com/b/bullying/

Higher Education Definitions

Grand Rapids Community College

Bullying is systematic intentional behavior that may take many forms, including but not limited to, repeated unwanted physical, verbal, or written acts which are hostile or offensive, targeted at an individual or group and creates an intimidating and/or threatening environment which produces a risk of psychological and/or physical harm. Bullying may manifest as cyber stalking or cyber bullying as well as excluding behaviors such as ignoring or dismissing individuals or groups.

1. Hostile behaviors include, but are not limited to, inappropriate behaviors that are harmful or damaging to an individual and/or property. Behaviors that are intimidating, threatening, disruptive, humiliating, sarcastic, or vicious may also constitute hostile behavior.
2. Offensive behaviors may include, but are not limited to, inappropriate behaviors such as abusive language, derogatory remarks, insults, or epithets. Other offensive behaviors may include the use of condescending, humiliating, or vulgar language, swearing, shouting or use of unsuitable language, use of obscene gestures, or mocking.

🕹 https://www.grcc.edu/studentlifeandconduct/studentconduct/codeofcon
duct/generalconduct

Tennessee State University

Bullying shall be defined as:

- Persistent singling out of one person.
- Repeatedly shouting or the raising of voice at an individual in public and/ or in private.
- Repeated and consistent public humiliation or reprimands in any form.
- Repeated criticism on matters unrelated or minimally related to the person's job performance or description.
- Repeatedly accusing someone of errors which are not documented.
- Spreading rumors or negative gossip about individuals.
- Encouraging others to disregard a manager's instructions.
- Manipulating the ability of someone to do their work (e.g., overloading, under-loading of work, withholding information, assigning meaningless tasks, knowingly setting deadlines that cannot be met, deliberately giving ambiguous instructions or supplying incorrect information) and encouraging others to collectively participate in these behaviors.
- Assigning menial or demeaning tasks, not in keeping with the normal responsibilities of the job as outlined in the job description.
- Refusing reasonable requests for leave without legitimate work-related justification.

It is important to recognize that bullying is distinguishable from supervisory activities in that bullying is a habitual pattern of intentional, socially damaging behavior designed to negatively impact a person's career or reputation. Behaviors that are not workplace bullying includes but are not limited to:

- Occasional conflict or disagreement.
- Being a demanding supervisor.
- Withholding resources for a legitimate reason.
- Holding staff accountable for clearly communicated job expectations.
- Consistent, appropriate and documented disciplinary action.

🕹 http://www.tnstate.edu/hr/documents/updatedpoliciesandprocedures/Code
%20of%20Ethical%20Conduct.pdf

Bennett College

Bullying behavior, defined as: the systematic and chronic infliction of physical hurt or psychological distress by teasing, social exclusion, threat, intimidation, stalking, physical violence, theft, harassment, or destruction of property.

Bullying may be intentional or unintentional. However, it must be noted that where an allegation of bullying is made, the intention of the alleged bully is irrelevant, and will not be given consideration when appropriate disciplinary action is needed.

Examples of bullying:

- Verbal Bullying: slandering, ridiculing or maligning a person or his/her family; persistent name calling which is hurtful, insulting or humiliating; using a person as the butt of jokes; remarks that would be viewed by others in the community as abusive and offensive; persistently interrupting another person or otherwise preventing another person's legitimate attempts to speak; use of nicknames after being warned that the nickname is considered by the victim to be offensive; constant criticism on matters unrelated to a person's job performance or description or on matters that cannot be documented;

- Physical Bullying: pushing; shoving; kicking; poking; tripping; assault, or threat of physical assault; damage to a person's work area or property

- Gesture Bullying: non-verbal threatening gestures, such as, but not limited to, the following: approaching another person with fists clinched or with one or more other fighting gestures which, could reasonably be interpreted as threatening; brandishing weapon; making gestures that would reasonably be interpreted as amorous or sexual in nature.

- Social Bullying (which may include Cyber-bullying): engaging in verbal bullying via mail, email, text message, phone, voicemail, or social media; deliberately interfering with mail, email, text messages, phone, voicemail or other communication; spreading malicious rumors or gossip about another person.

🕸 http://www.bennett.edu/wp-content/uploads/2017/02/Bennett_College_ Anti-Bullying_Policy_1-17-17.pdf

Gender

The concept of gender and use of the term is common in higher education websites, but a search of wide range of college and university websites provided no definitions of "gender." Because it is an important term in discussions of sexual harassment, however, two definitions of gender are provided from outside the academic world.

According to the World Health Organization, "Gender refers to the roles, behaviours [sic], activities, attributes and opportunities that any society considers appropriate for girls and boys, and women and men. Gender interacts with, but is different from, the binary categories of biological sex" (https://www.who .int/health-topics/gender).

Gender Spectrum provides a more nuanced definition:

> A person's gender is the complex interrelationship between three dimensions:
>
> - Body: our body, our experience of our own body, how society genders bodies, and how others interact with us based on our body.
> - Identity: the name we use to convey our gender based on our deeply held, internal sense of self. Identities typically fall into binary (e.g. man, woman), Non-binary (e.g. Genderqueer, genderfluid) and ungendered (e.g. Agender, genderless) categories; the meaning associated with a particular identity can vary among individuals using the same term. A person's Gender identity can correspond to or differ from the sex they were assigned at birth.
> - Social: how we present our gender in the world and how individuals, society, culture, and community perceive, interact with, and try to shape our gender. Social gender includes gender roles and expectations and how society uses those to try to enforce conformity to current gender norms.
>
> Each of these dimensions can vary greatly across a range of possibilities and is distinct from, but interrelated with the others. A person's comfort in their gender is related to the degree to which these three dimensions feel in harmony.

🌐 https://www.genderspectrum.org/quick-links/understanding-gender/

Hostile Work Environment

Not unlike bullying, a hostile work environment may not be due to sexual harassment alone. Hostile work environment is included here because it can accompany sexual harassment.

Popular Press Understanding

The legal requirements for a hostile work environment include these.

- The actions or behavior must discriminate against a protected classification such as age, religion, disability, or race.
- The behavior or communication must be pervasive, lasting over time, and not limited to an off-color remark or two that a coworker found annoying. These incidents should be reported to Human Resources for needed intervention.

- The problem becomes significant and pervasive if it is all around a worker, continues over time, and is not investigated and addressed effectively enough by the organization to make the behavior stop.
- The hostile behavior, actions, or communication must be severe. Not only is it pervasive over time, but the hostility must seriously disrupt the employee's work. The second form of severity occurs if the hostile work environment interferes with an employee's career progress; for example, if the employee failed to receive a promotion or a job rotation as a result of the hostile behavior.
- It is reasonable to assume that the employer knew about the actions or behavior and did not sufficiently intervene. Consequently, the employer can be liable for the creation of a hostile work environment.

🌐 https://www.thebalancecareers.com/what-makes-a-work-environment-hostile-1919363

Legal Resource Definition

The phrase hostile work environment is a civil law term that refers to the behavior of an individual in a workplace that creates an environment that makes work difficult or uncomfortable for another person. This includes behavior that may leave another employee feeling afraid or violated. Such offensive behavior happens in many forms, including sexual harassment.

When an individual in the workplace feels scared, intimidated, or uncomfortable due to abuse or intimidation by a coworker, it creates what is called a hostile work environment. While any number of behaviors might create a hostile work environment, any conduct or actions that create an environment in which an employee dreads going to work is generally seen to create such a setting.

A hostile work environment is sometimes referred to as an "offensive work environment," or an "abusive work environment." The individual causing a hostile work environment may be an employee, a supervisor, an owner, or even and independent contractor. There are federal and state laws in place to protect employees from being subjected to workplace hostility.

🌐 https://legaldictionary.net/hostile-work-environment/

Higher Education Definitions

Norfolk State University

A "hostile environment" exists when the conduct is sufficiently severe, persistent, or pervasive that it unreasonably interferes with, limits, or deprives an individual from participating in or benefitting from NSU's education or employment programs and/or activities. Conduct must be deemed severe, persistent, or pervasive from both a subjective and an objective perspective. In evaluating whether a hostile environment exists, NSU will consider the totality of known circumstances, including, but not limited to:

- The frequency, nature and severity of the conduct;
- Whether the conduct was physically threatening;
- The effect of the conduct on the Complainant's mental or emotional state;
- Whether the conduct was directed at more than one person;
- Whether the conduct arose in the context of other discriminatory conduct;
- Whether the conduct unreasonably interfered with the Complainant's educational or work performance and/or NSU programs or activities; and
- Whether the conduct implicates concerns related to academic freedom or protected speech.

A hostile environment can be created by persistent or pervasive conduct or by a single or isolated incident, if sufficiently severe. The more severe the conduct, the less need there is to show a repetitive series of incidents to prove a hostile environment, particularly if the conduct is physical. A single incident of Sexual Assault, for example, may be sufficiently severe to constitute a hostile environment. In contrast, the perceived offensiveness of a single verbal or written expression, standing alone, is typically not sufficient to constitute a hostile environment.

🌐 https://www.nsu.edu/policy/bov-05.aspx

Missouri State University

A "hostile work environment" is created when sexual harassment is sufficiently severe or pervasive as to disrupt a person's ability to participate in educational programs or the workplace.

🌐 https://www.missouristate.edu/policy/Op1_02_8_Harassment.htm

Utica College

Hostile environment sexual harassment involves a situation where an atmosphere or climate is created on the campus that makes it difficult, if not impossible, for a student to learn or an employee to work because the atmosphere is perceived by the employee or student to be intimidating, offensive, and hostile. The fact that a person was personally offended by a statement or incident does not alone constitute a violation of this policy. A determination as to whether a hostile environment has been created is based on a "reasonable person" standard and takes into account the totality of the circumstances, such as the severity of the particular incident, the context in which it occurred, the relationship of the individuals involved, whether the conduct was an isolated incident or part of a broader pattern or course of offensive conduct, whether the conduct was verbal or physical, and whether it was threatening or merely annoying.

The College reserves the right to discipline offensive conduct that is inconsistent with community standards even if it does not rise to the level of a hostile environment as defined by applicable law. Further, the College encourages individuals to report incidents that concern them even if the incidents are not particularly egregious, as early reporting assists the College in addressing and even correcting situations before they become so severe or pervasive as to create a hostile environment.

🦚 https://www.utica.edu/policies/policies.cfm?id=145

Mandatory Reporting

Mandatory reporting requirements are included in Title IV, but they have created considerable controversy. Aspects of that controversy were outlined in a 2017 *Academe* article by Sine Anahita. Recounting an experience that many teachers have encountered, Anahita commented,

> Okay, you might say, forewarn students that faculty are mandatory reporters and that they should not confide in us if they do not want to be reported. But it's not that simple. The student's e-mail is already in my inbox. The written assignment is already submitted online. The student has already confided to me in my office. It's too late. I already know. And I must report the student or be fired." (https://www.aaup.org/article/trouble-title-ix#.XTi FEfi7kbi, Para. 3)

Despite the controversy, a thorough review of institutional websites indicated that all have some mandatory reporting policy.

Popular Press Understanding

In many parts of the western world, **mandated reporters** are people who have regular contact with vulnerable people and are therefore legally required to ensure a report is made when abuse is observed or suspected. Specific details vary across jurisdictions—the abuse that must be reported may include neglect, or financial, physical, sexual, or other types of abuse. Mandated reporters may include paid or unpaid people who have assumed full or intermittent responsibility for the care of a child, dependent adult, or elder.

🦚 https://en.wikipedia.org/wiki/Mandated_reporter

Legal Resource Definition

Title IX of the Higher Education Amendments of 1972 (Title IX) specifies that any educational institution receiving federal funding must prevent sex-based discrimination and respond to acts of sexual discrimination when they do occur [4].

In April 2011, the Office of Civil Rights released a Dear Colleague Letter, which provided specific guidance on schools' duties to ensure that sexual assault and harassment are properly addressed in educational settings [5]. In particular, this letter explained that universities are obligated to take action in response to sexual violence if any university employees who are not confidential employees (e.g., student health providers, victim services advocates) know of the incident [6]. Specifically, university employees are required to report incidents of sexual violence involving students to the Title IX coordinator. It should be noted that prior to the April 2011 Dear Colleague Letter, Title IX requirements were primarily interpreted through case law [4].

🌐 https://www.ncbi.nlm.nih.gov/pmc/articles/PMC6262634/#B4-behavsci-08 -00106

Higher Education Definitions

Moberly Area Community College

Responsible Employees (Mandated Reporters)

All MACC employees are considered responsible employees (i.e., mandated reporters), and as such are expected to promptly contact the Title IX Coordinator when they become aware of an incident of sexual misconduct, regardless of whether the recipient is an employee, a student, a volunteer, or a visitor of the College.

When an individual tells a responsible employee about an incident of sexual misconduct, the individual has the right to expect the College to take immediate and appropriate steps to investigate what happened and to resolve the matter promptly and equitably. To the extent possible, information reported to a responsible employee will be shared only with people responsible for handling the College's response to the report. These people will include the Title IX Coordinator and may include the College's Behavioral Intervention Team, administrative council, and/or the Director of Security and Residential Life. A responsible employee should not share information with law enforcement without the complainant's consent or unless the complainant has also reported the incident to law enforcement.

Before an individual reveals any information about sexual misconduct to a responsible employee, the employee should ensure that the individual understands the employee's reporting obligations, and, if the individual wants to maintain confidentiality, direct the individual to confidential resources. If the individual wants to tell the responsible employee what happened but also maintain confidentiality, the employee should tell the individual that the College will consider the request but cannot guarantee that the College will be able to honor it. In reporting the details of the incident to the Title IX Coordinator, the responsible employee will also inform the Coordinator of the individual's request for confidentiality. Responsible employees will not pressure an individual to request confidentiality but will honor and support the individual's wishes, including the wish that the College fully investigate an incident. Responsible employees will not pressure an individual to make a full report if the individual is not ready to.

Should the Title IX Coordinator be given information by a third party or an anonymous person, the details will be discussed with the alleged victim if that name is given. The alleged victim will make the determination if he or she wants to provide details regarding the incident. Even if the individual does not choose to participate in the reporting process, the information given by the third party will be documented. Under no circumstances should anyone involved in the reporting of a crime be a victim of retaliation. MACC prohibits retaliation and will take strong responsive action if retaliation occurs.

Weighing Requests for Confidentiality

If an individual discloses an incident to a responsible employee but wishes to maintain confidentiality or requests that no investigation into a particular incident be conducted or disciplinary action taken, the College must weigh that request against the College's obligation to provide a safe, non-discriminatory environment for all students, employees, and visitors. If the College honors the request for confidentiality, a complainant must understand that the College's ability to meaningfully investigate the incident and pursue disciplinary action against the respondent(s), if appropriate, may be limited. Although rare, there are times when the College may not be able to honor an individual's request in order to provide a safe, non-discriminatory environment for all students, employees, and visitors.

The Director of Security and Residential Life will evaluate requests for confidentiality. When weighing a complainant's request for confidentiality or that no investigation or discipline be pursued, the Director of Security and Residential Life will consider a range of factors, including the safety of the College community, the age of the complainant(s) and respondent(s), and the seriousness of the allegations. If the College determines that it cannot maintain an individual's confidentiality, the College will inform the complainant prior to starting an investigation and will, to the extent possible, only share information with people responsible for handling the College's response. The College will remain ever mindful of the complainant's well-being and will take ongoing steps to protect the individual from retaliation or harm and work with the complainant to create a safety plan. Retaliation against the complainant, whether by students, employees, or other College representatives will not be tolerated. If the College determines that it can respect a complainant's request for confidentiality, the College will also take immediate action as necessary to protect and assist the complainant (e.g., rearrange living assignments, work schedules, and/or class schedules if at all possible, etc.).

The information reported to the Title IX Coordinator may also be used (without the victim's name) to issue timely warnings, which are required by the Clery Act. If applicable, the incident must be reported in the Annual Security Report (anonymously, as a statistic), which is also mandated by the Clery Act.

MACC encourages victims of sexual misconduct to talk about their experience so they get the support they need and so officials can respond appropriately. Should an individual decide not to pursue the incident by criminal or institutional processes, an individual can and should contact a confidential source to seek guidance.

Professional licensed counselors and pastoral counselors as well as non-professional counselors and advocates who provide mental health counseling or services to members of the school community (and including those who act in that role under the supervision of a licensed counselor) are not required to report any information about an incident to the Title IX Coordinator without a victim's permission. MACC does not offer on-site professional or pastoral counseling services; however, these confidential services are available off-site through the College's Employee/Student Assistance Program or through community agencies, such as those identified in Section V of this policy.

An individual who speaks to a professional counselor or advocate must understand that, if the individual wants to maintain confidentiality, the College will be unable to conduct an investigation into the particular incident or pursue disciplinary action against the respondent. An individual who at first requests confidentiality may later decide to file a complaint with the College or report the incident to local law enforcement and thus have the incident fully investigated.

🔗 https://www.macc.edu/sexual-misconduct-policy#iv-reporting-and-confi dentiality

Columbia University

Prohibited Conduct That Involves Students

When prohibited conduct involves students, there are additional reporting obligations. The following employees have a duty to report any instance or allegation of prohibited conduct involving a student that is disclosed to, observed, or otherwise known by him or her whether the student is a Complainant or a Respondent:

- Faculty, Officers of Administration, Research, the Libraries and the Coaching Staff
- Staff who work directly with students, including teaching assistants, advising and residential program staff (including residence assistants and student affairs staff).Prohibited conduct should be reported immediately to the appropriate individual identified in the chart under Appendix A.

Prohibited Conduct by Employees or Third Parties That Does Not Involve Students

The University asks all employees to report any prohibited conduct involving employees or third parties to EOAA and/or the employee's designated human resources representative. The University requires management and supervisory personnel to report any instance or allegation of prohibited conduct by an employee or third party that is disclosed to, observed, or otherwise known by him or her to EOAA and/or his or her designated human resources representative, who will report to immediately and coordinate with EOAA regarding the appropriate University response.

Failure of a manager or supervisor to report an allegation of prohibited conduct disclosed to, observed or otherwise known by him or her will constitute a violation of this Policy and may result in disciplinary action, even in situations where the University determines that the underlying conduct does not constitute a policy violation.

🌐 https://eoaa.columbia.edu/sites/default/files/content/docs/EOAA_Policy _10_03_2018.pdf

Texas Women's University

Texas Woman's University is committed to eliminating sexual misconduct and to providing support to any individual who has been a target of sexual misconduct. Because of this commitment and as called for by Title IX of the Education Amendments of 1972, all faculty members and graduate assistants must report any instance of sexual misconduct that you disclose in the course of discussion or an assignment. Title IX places no time limit on our need to report a violation. Therefore, if you disclose experiences such as sexual harassment, sexual assault, stalking, or relationship violence which occurred during your studies at TWU, then we must report this to the University's Title IX Coordinator to determine whether further action is necessary.

🌐 https://servicecenter.twu.edu/TDClient/KB/ArticleDet?ID=71188

Microaggressions

No university or college was found to have an explicit or specific policy regarding "microaggressions." Many colleges and universities have discussion links, workshops, forums, and study guides about microaggressions and how to mitigate and manage them. In fact, at Harvard in 2018, reports of microaggressions in seven classes in the School of Public Health led to those courses being "flagged for special review and attention" (Vrotsos, para. 5).

Popular Press Understanding

Behaviors or statements that do not necessarily reflect malicious intent but which nevertheless can inflict insult or injury.

🜚 https://www.theatlantic.com/politics/archive/2015/09/microaggressions -matter/406090/

Legal Resource Definition

Due to their subtle nature, microaggressions are often challenging to address, but they can strain working relationships. Left unaddressed, microaggressions can over time lead to workplace conflict and eventually affect operations. Additionally, severe or pervasive microaggressions based on protected Equal Employment Opportunity categories may rise to the level of harassment under certain circumstances.

🜚 https://2009-2017.state.gov/documents/organization/249252.pdf

Quid Pro Quo

Latin for "something for something," quid pro quo is perhaps one of the best-known types of sexual harassment. Being well-known, however, is no protection against its insidious effects.

Popular Press Understanding

"It's the kind that is seen in pop culture, splashed across television screens and nestled into iconic cinematic scenes." This site generally defines quid pro quo as a superior "taking advantage of their power over an individual and demanding sexual favors for job benefit.

🜚 https://fairygodboss.com/career-topics/quid-pro-quo-sexual-harassment

Legal Resource Definition

Quid pro quo harassment occurs in the workplace when a manager or other authority figure offers or merely hints that he or she will give the employee something (a raise or a promotion) in return for that employee's satisfaction of a sexual demand. This also occurs when a manager or other authority figure says he or she will not fire or reprimand an employee in exchange for some type of sexual favor. A job applicant also may be the subject of this kind of harassment if the hiring decision was based on the acceptance or rejection of sexual advances.

🜚 http://employment.findlaw.com/employment-discrimination/what-is-quid -pro-quo-harassment.html

Higher Education Definitions

Spelman College

Quid pro quo Sexual Harassment occurs when a person having power or authority over another makes unwelcome sexual advances, requests for sexual favors, and other verbal or physical conduct of a sexual nature and makes submission to such sexual conduct either explicitly or implicitly a term or condition of rating or evaluating an individual's educational [or employment] progress, development, or performance. This includes making submission to such conduct a condition for access to receiving the benefits of any educational [or employment] program.

Examples of quid pro quo harassment include: an attempt to coerce an unwilling person into a sexual relationship; repeatedly subjecting a person to egregious, unwelcome sexual attention; punishing a refusal to comply with a sexual based request; conditioning a benefit on submitting to sexual advances; sexual violence; intimate partner violence; stalking; gender-based bullying.

🌐 https://www.spelman.edu/docs/title-ix/sexual-misconduct-policy.pdf

Harvard University

Sexual harassment is unwelcome conduct of a sexual nature, including unwelcome sexual advances, requests for sexual favors, and other verbal, nonverbal, graphic, or physical conduct of a sexual nature, when: (1) submission to or rejection of such conduct is made either explicitly or implicitly a condition of an individual's employment or academic standing or is used as the basis for employment decisions or for academic evaluation, grades, or advancement (quid pro quo). . . . Quid pro quo sexual harassment can occur whether a person resists and suffers the threatened harm, or the person submits and avoids the threatened harm. Both situations could constitute discrimination on the basis of sex.

🌐 https://www.hupd.harvard.edu/sexual-and-gender-based-harassment-policy

Brigham Young University

Quid pro quo sexual harassment—when submission to or rejection of the unwelcome sexual conduct is used as a basis for employment decisions affecting an employee, or when a teacher or other employee conditions an educational decision or benefit on a student's submission to unwelcome sexual conduct.

To avoid the possibility or appearance of quid pro quo sexual harassment, employees and students should avoid dating, romantic, or amorous relationships where a power differential exists.

🌐 https://policy.byu.edu/view/index.php?p=155

Rape

Whether or not to include rape in these definitions was carefully considered by the authors. It seemed obvious that rape was sexual harassment, but definitions of rape are not as clear and uniform as might be expected. Ultimately, the variety of definitions discovered argued convincingly for the term's inclusion.

Popular Press Understanding

What is rape? Rape is a form of sexual assault, but not all sexual assault is rape. The term rape is often used as a legal definition to specifically include sexual penetration without consent.

🌐 https://www.rainn.org/articles/sexual-assault

Legal Resource Definition

United States Department of Justice

The penetration, no matter how slight, of the vagina or anus with any body part or object, or oral penetration by a sex organ of another person, without the consent of the victim.

🌐 https://www.justice.gov/archives/opa/blog/updated-definition-rape

Higher Education Definitions

Langston University

Rape is nonconsensual intercourse that involves the threat of force, violence, immediate and unlawful bodily injury, or threat of future retaliation and duress. http://www.langston.edu/title-ix/defining-terms

University of Pennsylvania

Rape is defined as sexual assault involving an act of penetration and includes acquaintance rape (assailant and victim know each other).

🌐 https://almanac.upenn.edu/archive/volumes/v60/n35/sexualviolencepolicy.html

Grand Valley State University

Rape is sexual penetration, however slight, of another person without affirmative consent. Penetration can be of the mouth, vagina, or anus, and can be with a penis, tongue, finger, or foreign object.

🌐 https://www.gvsu.edu/policies/policy.htm?policyId=145A3666-BB0D-3BC0-EC121EFDF110009B&search=sexual

College of the Ozarks

Rape or sexual assault: sexual intercourse (anal, oral, or vaginal) by a man or woman upon a man or woman without consent.

🌐 http://images.cofo.edu/cofo/TitleIXPolicyProcedures1114.pdf

Retaliation

Fear of retaliation is one of the most common reasons sexual harassment is not reported. For that reason, everyone in higher education should know the policies in place to prevent the additional trauma that retaliation can bring.

Popular Press Understanding

Retaliation is an act of revenge or reprisal.

🌐 https://www.thebalancecareers.com/retaliation-is-illegal-1917921

Legal Resource Definition

Retaliation is the most frequently alleged basis of discrimination in the federal sector and the most common discrimination finding in federal sector cases. Common retaliation against an employee occurs as a result to then employee "resisting sexual advances, or intervening to protect others."

🌐 https://www.eeoc.gov/laws/types/retaliation.cfm

Higher Education Definitions

Hagerstown Community College

Retaliation means intimidating, threatening, coercing, or discriminating against any individual for the purpose of interfering with any right or privilege secured by law or College policy relating to Sexual Assault/Misconduct, or because an individual has made a report, testified, assisted, or participated in any manner in an investigation, proceeding, or hearing related to Sexual Assault/Misconduct. Retaliation includes retaliatory harassment. (par. 12)

🌐 http://www.hagerstowncc.edu/student-affairs/sexual-misconduct-proce dures

University of Montana

Retaliation is action taken by an accused individual or an action taken by a third party against any person because that person has opposed any practices forbidden under this policy or because that person has filed a complaint, testified, assisted, or participated in any manner in an investigation or proceeding under this policy. This includes action taken against a bystander who intervened to stop or attempt to stop discrimination, harassment, or sexual misconduct. Retaliation includes intimidating, threatening, coercing, or in any way discriminating against an individual because of the individual's complaint or participation. Action is generally deemed retaliatory if it would deter a reasonable person in the same circumstances from opposing practices prohibited by this policy.

🕏 http://www.umt.edu/policies/browse/personnel/discrimination-harassment
   -sexual-misconduct-stalking-and-retaliation

Seton Hall University

Retaliation is an act of intimidation, harassment, or reprisal against an individual for initiating a good faith complaint or participating in any proceeding under this policy or for otherwise exercising his/her rights under this policy or the law.

🕏 http://www.shu.edu/policies/policy-against-sexual-misconduct-harassment
   -and-retaliation.cfm

Sexual Assault

The term *sexual assault* is an unhelpful term if precision in discussion is a goal. The term is a capacious canopy that is used to cover issues that should be more carefully delineated.

Popular Press Understanding

Sexual assault is basically an umbrella term that includes sexual activities such as rape, fondling, and attempted rape.

🕏 https://www.self.com/story/sexual-assault-definition

Legal Resource Definition

The United States Department of Justice defines sexual assault as "any nonconsensual sexual act proscribed by Federal, tribal, or State law, including when the victim lacks capacity to consent."

🕏 https://www.justice.gov/ovw/sexual-assault

Higher Education Definitions

Howard University

Sexual assault is sexual contact without consent. No one is immune to sexual assault, no deserves it, and no one asks for it. Sexual assault may include unwanted sexual touching, rape, attempted rape, or otherwise forcing a person to perform sexual acts.

🌐 https://studentaffairs.howard.edu/addressing-sexual-assault

New Mexico State University

Sexual assault can include many other definitions, but as a whole, can be defined as unwanted sexual contact that stops short of rape or attempted rape. This includes sexual touching and fondling.

Forms of sexual assault can include the following:

- Sexual Contact: Any unwanted touching to the intimate parts underneath the clothes of someone who is eighteen years of age, or intentionally causing this person to touch one's intimate parts.
- Sexual Coercion: Forcing someone to engage in something they do not want to do.
- Attempted Rape: An attempt to complete criminal sexual penetration the victim.
- Rape or Criminal Sexual Penetration: "The unlawful and intentional causing of a person to engage in sexual intercourse, cunnilingus, fellatio, or anal intercourse, or the causing of penetration to any extent and with any object, of the genital or anal openings of another, whether or not there is any emission.

🌐 https://wave.nmsu.edu/violence/sexual-assault/

Loyola Marymount University

Sexual assault includes rape, statutory rape, rape in concert, sodomy, oral copulation and penetration of the vagina or anal opening by any foreign object.

🌐 https://studentaffairs.lmu.edu/wellness/lmucares/aboutlmucares/state federallaws/

Stalking

Before the term was used as a type of sexual harassment, "to stalk" meant to creep up stealthy on prey. It was often used to describe how a cat follows a bird. Perhaps its contemporary meaning is not so different.

Popular Press Understanding

To follow and/or spy on someone you have feelings for. Those feelings need not be of a kind and loving nature. People who stalk are usually obsessed with the stalkee.

⊕ https://www.urbandictionary.com/define.php?term=Stalking

Legal Resource Definition

The crime of stalking can be simply described as the unwanted pursuit of another person. Examples of this type of behavior includes following a person, appearing at a person's home or place of business, making harassing phone calls, leaving written messages or objects, or vandalizing a person's property.

⊕ https://criminal.findlaw.com/criminal-charges/stalking.html

Higher Education Definitions

Danville Area Community College

Stalking is committed when a person (a) engages in a course of conduct directed at a specific person, and the conduct would cause that person to fear for his or her safety or the safety of another, or suffer other emotional distress; (b) follows/observes a person on at least two separate occasions and transmits a threat, or causes fear of bodily harm, sexual assault, confinement, or restraint of that person or a family member; or (c) has previously been convicted of stalking and on one occasion follows/observes that same person and transmits a threat of bodily harm, sexual assault, confinement, or restraint to that person or a family member. Stalking may include spying on the target; sending unwanted presents; spreading rumors; damaging the target's property or defaming the target's character; and/or unwanted calls, emails, text messages and instant messages.

⊕ https://www.dacc.edu/title-ix/definitions

Brown University

Stalking occurs when a person engages in a course of conduct toward another person under circumstances that would cause a person to fear bodily injury or experience substantial emotional distress.

Course of conduct means two or more instances including but not limited to unwelcome acts in which the stalker directly, indirectly, or through third parties, by any action, method, device, or means, follows, monitors, observes, surveils, threatens, or communicates to or about a person, or interferes with a person's property. Substantial emotional distress means significant mental suffering or anguish.

Stalking includes the concept of cyber-stalking, a particular form of stalking in which electronic media such as the internet, social networks, blogs, cell phones, texts, or other similar devices or forms of contact are used.

⊕ https://www.brown.edu/about/administration/title-ix/policy

Barnard College

Stalking means a course of conduct directed at a specific person that would cause a reasonable person to feel fear for her, his or others' safety or to suffer substantial emotional distress. Stalking involves repeated and continued behaviors that may include: pursuing or following; non-consensual (unwanted) communication or contact—including face-to-face, telephone calls, voice messages, electronic messages, text messages, unwanted gifts or tokens; trespassing; and surveillance or other types of observation.

(🌐) https://barnard.edu/doc/titleix/definitions

Title VII

Title VII prohibits employment discrimination based on race, color, religion, sex and national origin. The Civil Rights Act of 1991 (Pub. L. 102–166) (CRA) and the Lily Ledbetter Fair Pay Act of 2009 (Pub. L. 111–2) amend several sections of Title VII. In addition, section 102 of the CRA . . . amends the Revised Statutes by adding a new section following section 1977 (42 U.S.C. 1981), to provide for the recovery of compensatory and punitive damages in cases of intentional violations of Title VII, the Americans with Disabilities Act of 1990, and section 501 of the Rehabilitation Act of 1973.

(🌐) https://www.eeoc.gov/laws/statutes/titlevii.cfm

Title VII of the Civil Rights Act of 1964, as amended, protects applicants and employees from discrimination in hiring, promotion, discharge, pay, fringe benefits, job training, classification, referral, and other aspects of employment, on the basis of race, color, religion, sex (including pregnancy), or national origin. Religious discrimination includes failing to reasonably accommodate an employee's religious practices where the accommodation does not impose undue hardship.

(🌐) https://www.eeoc.gov/employers/upload/poster_screen_reader_optimized.pdf

Title IX

The U.S. Department of Education's Office for Civil Rights (OCR) enforces, among other statutes, Title IX of the Education Amendments of 1972. Title IX protects people from discrimination based on sex in education programs or activities that receive Federal financial assistance. Title IX states that:

No person in the United States shall, on the basis of sex, be excluded from participation in, be denied the benefits of, or be subjected to discrimination under any education program or activity receiving Federal financial assistance.

Scope of Title IX

Title IX applies to institutions that receive federal financial assistance from ED, including state and local educational agencies. These agencies include approximately 16,500 local school districts, 7,000 postsecondary institutions, as well as charter schools, for-profit schools, libraries, and museums. Also included are vocational rehabilitation agencies and education agencies of 50 states, the District of Columbia, and territories and possessions of the United States.

Educational programs and activities that receive ED funds must operate in a nondiscriminatory manner. Some key issue areas in which recipients have Title IX obligations are: recruitment, admissions, and counseling; financial assistance; athletics; sex-based harassment; treatment of pregnant and parenting students; discipline; single-sex education; and employment. Also, a recipient may not retaliate against any person for opposing an unlawful educational practice or policy, or made charges, testified or participated in any complaint action under Title IX. For a recipient to retaliate in any way is considered a violation of Title IX. The ED Title IX regulations (Volume 34, Code of Federal Regulations, Part 106) provide additional information about the forms of discrimination prohibited by Title IX.

🜚 https://www2.ed.gov/about/offices/list/ocr/docs/tix_dis.html?exp=0

Chapter 3: Baking It In

Patricia Freitag Ericsson
WASHINGTON STATE UNIVERSITY

According to Claire Cain Miller, who won a Pulitzer Prize writing about sexual harassment, "The best way to avoid sexual harassment and ensure that it's reported when it happens is to *bake it into company culture* [emphasis added]" (2017, para. 23). This chapter, and this book, is built on that premise—that sexual harassment prevention needs to be baked into the culture of higher education, but more specifically for this book, baked into the culture of writing studies programs.

Institutional culture, a shared system of beliefs, values, and assumptions, is malleable, but cannot be changed by a one-shot inoculation. Baking sexual harassment prevention into a culture demands a multifaceted approach. This approach is a "transactional" one that requires leadership that Elaine P. Maimon (2018) described as "more focused on relationships, more open to multiple interpretations, more adaptable to new situations, more flexible in adjusting to new environments, readier to multitask, and capable of paying attention both to the goals themselves and to the process for achieving those goals" (p. 5). To promote transactional culture-changing this chapter considers three approaches to sexual harassment prevention: 1) Hiring and promoting more women, 2) Creating a culture of reporting, 3) Instituting effective sexual harassment training through active bystander training and interactive scenario training. These approaches are not the only ways to tackle the problem, but are ones that have strong potential to work, especially in writing studies.

Hiring and Promoting More Women

High profile people from Cheryl Sandberg to Barack Obama have argued that having more women in positions of power will make women less vulnerable to sexual harassment. In a 2017 Facebook post, Facebook CEO Cheryl Sandberg wrote, "Ultimately, the thing that will bring the most to change our culture is the one I've been writing and talking about for a long time: having more women with more power" (para. 16). Speaking at a 2017 Paris gathering, former President Obama opined that more women were needed in positions of power because "men seem to be having some problems these days" (Mazza, para. 2). There is no doubt that Sandberg's interest in cultural change is appropriate, and Obama's observation is undeniably accurate. However, research into this approach has not always shown positive results. In their research, McLaughlin, Uggen, and Blackstone (2012) concluded, "For women who become bosses, their positions create

DOI: https://doi.org/10.37514/PRA-B.2020.0988.2.03

a paradox of power in a gender system that continues to subordinate women. In taking on positions of authority, they also take on a greater risk of sexual harassment" (p. 642). This same research argued, "Women supervisors, who hold authority over some men, directly challenge the presumptive superiority of men" (p. 627). Sexual harassment is too often used as the equalizer against women in positions of power.

Harassment is more likely if a woman is outnumbered in power situations. The promotion of a few isolated women as part of the baking-it-in-to-the-culture remedy is likely to be an ineffective solution. The remedy lies partly in having enough women in positions of power and authority to have collective power. McLaughlin stated, "I do think that there is safety in numbers" (Zillman, 2017, para. 12).

Numbers favor women in writing studies. Combined numbers of the Two Year and Four Year Studies of The National Census of Writing (2014) survey found all types of writing programs at both 2-year and 4-year institutions were led by women by a 2/1 margin (633 leaders of writing programs identified as female; 323 identified as male, and 6 identified as other). Sadly, these numbers do not always guarantee less sexual harassment or timely action when incidents are reported. Recently, Michelle Graber (2018) argued, "Female administrators, too, can be complicit in the acceptance of harassment" (p. 197). Female writing studies administrators may find themselves needing to "prove" themselves to the largely male administrative upper echelons. Gaining acceptance in these levels may demand that women enact "hegemonic masculinity" which researchers assert "operates through collective practice" (McLaughlin, et al., 2012, p. 636). Instead of working against hegemonic masculinity, female administrators may find themselves co-opted by it. Becoming part of this misogynistic culture can give female administrators *entrée* to a power status that fighting against this culture denies.

In the academic world, the concept idea of safety in numbers may not always hold in feminized disciplines like writing studies. Safety will come when the male-dominated upper administration is more fully gender-equal and when the bonds of hegemonic masculinity are broken. All those working in writing studies (women and men alike) can demand a voice in hiring discussions and suggest and amplify women candidates, especially in hiring at higher administrative levels where more women are sorely needed. Women who move from writing studies to other administrative positions can stay aware of hegemonic masculinity and work to undermine it, not be tempted by the power that cooperating with it may bring.

Creating a Culture of Reporting

"Baking it in" is an impossible goal without changing the current culture of non-reporting. The 2016 EEOC "Task Force on the Study of Harassment in the Workplace" showed that "Roughly three out of four individuals who experienced harassment never even talked to a supervisor, manager, or union representative about the harassing conduct" (Feldblum & Lipnic, p. 6). In addition, the report concluded, "anywhere from 87% to 94% of individuals did *not* file a formal complaint" (p. 23).

In her 2018 article about sexual harassment, feminist scholar Margaret E. Johnson laid out additional information on sexual harassment non-reporting maintaining, "barely 1 in 4 ever do [report]" (para. 4). Johnson indicated three legal barriers to reporting including 1) limited legal definitions of sexual harassment, 2) employers being legally shielded from liability in these cases, and 3) legal complications surrounding retaliation. Other research has noted that in addition to the legal concerns, victims fear they will face disbelief, inaction, blame, or societal and professional retaliation.

Academic organizations and institutions report similar levels of non-reporting. The 2017 *AAU Campus Climate Survey Report* concluded that 25% or fewer of "even the most serious incidents are reported to an organization or agency (e.g., Title IX office; law enforcement)" (p. 50). A 2017 University of Texas Report, *Learning and Safe Environments*, found "The majority of victims of sexual harassment, stalking, dating/domestic abuse and violence and unwanted sexual contact (72%) did not disclose to anyone about the incident prior to taking this survey." Of the 28% who disclosed at all, only 8% of those reported to someone at a UT institution. (p. 57)

In addition to the legal complications in reporting, the 2017 AAU report indicated that for students "the dominant reason [for non-reporting] was that it [the harassment] was not considered serious enough" (p. xxi). The report went on "Even for penetration involving physical force, over half (8.6%) of students gave this reason" (p. xxi). Other significant reasons for non-reporting included embarrassment, shame, or emotional difficulty. And not surprisingly, many students claimed they "did not think anything would be done about it." (p. 50). The Texas report found that of the students who had disclosed sexual harassment before the study itself, only 6% had disclosed to any university institutional office (p. 52).

To promote a culture of reporting, the process of reporting needs to be a known rather than a worrisome unknown. In the AAU Report, 25.8% of students knew where to make a report of sexual harassment. In contrast, however, only 11.4% knew what happened after a report is made (p. 47–48). The overall lack of knowledge about the reporting process deters reporting.

Two human resource (HR) professionals who participated anonymously in research for this chapter weighed in on reporting. Respondent A (personal communication, November 2018) stated, "There should not be fear of reporting. That often requires a culture shift and someone who is trusted being in the position to be the intake person." In addition, this respondent acknowledged, "All complainants should understand what will happen once they make a complaint. This procedure should be clearly stated on a website and/or in a pamphlet, etc." Respondent B (personal communication, January 2019) confirmed this, adding,

"It is important that higher ed. organizations create a culture of reporting. . . . Organizations must encourage all their employees that even when in doubt any incident reported to them should be brought to the attention of the leaders."

In order to build a culture of reporting, both of these HR professionals strongly encouraged reporting. Respondent B urged, "Report it immediately. Even when in doubt, report it." Respondent A was equally emphatic, saying, "Do something about it. Talk to a trusted person to move forward with a complaint about the situation. It will not go away on its own."

The American Association of University Women (2019) provides a "What Should I Do Next" guide that suggests steps for reporting sexual harassment. Briefly, those include 1) consulting your institution's guidelines, 2) reporting the behavior to a supervisor or other trusted person in the institution, 3) confiding in family, friends, and coworkers, and 4) contacting the EEOC (if desired). Embedded in these actions is another crucial step in the process, "Take immediate notes on the harassment and be specific in your details—note the time and place of each incident, what was said and done, and who witnessed the actions" (Step 1). AAUW strongly promotes a culture of reporting, emphasizing the bravery it takes to so do, "The courageous act of reporting can change your employment culture and help to create more inclusive social norms at work" (Sidebar 1).

Instituting Effective Sexual Harassment Prevention Training

Sexual harassment prevention training is widespread throughout U.S. higher education largely because law requires it. According to a 2018 report, *Sexual Harassment of Women* by the National Academy of Sciences, Engineering, and Medicine, "Too often, judicial interpretation of Title IX and Title VII has incentivized institutions to create policies and training on sexual harassment that focus on symbolic compliance with current law and avoiding liability, and not on preventing sexual harassment" (Johnson, Widnall & Benya, p. 2). Readers who have experienced institutional sexual harassment training can validate that many training programs provide just enough to limit an institution's liability, but not enough to create meaningful cultural change.

The same report noted that studies of sexual harassment training effectiveness are "sparse," but the ones that have been done found "trainings can improve knowledge of policies and awareness of what is sexual harassment; however, trainings have either no effect or a negative effect on preventing sexual harassment" (p. 151). In other words, exposure to the legal ramifications of sexual harassment is not enough. The report concluded, "effort seems better spent on developing and using sexual harassment trainings aimed at changing people's behaviors rather than on their attitudes and beliefs" (p. 151). Two approaches to training that have shown promise in promoting cultural change are Bystander Training and Interactive Scenario Training.

Bystander Training

In the popular vernacular, a "bystander" is witness to an event but does not participate in the event. Criminology and social psychology research, however, has developed theories that split bystanders into categories. The "passive bystander" is the witness who does not participate in an event. According to MIT's Active Bystander website, "an active bystander takes steps that can make a difference" (2004, para. 3).

Bystander training was mandated in the 2013 Campus Sexual Violence Elimination Act which requires programming that teaches "safe and positive options for bystander intervention that may be carried out by an individual to prevent harm or intervene when there is a risk of domestic violence, dating violence, sexual assault, or stalking against a person other than such individual" (Section 2 (dd)). This Act covers all types of sexual harassment. Not surprisingly, passage of this Act created a flurry of Bystander Training development as well as research into those programs. To meet the requirements of this Act, many institutions use one of two proprietary programs: Green Dot and Bringing in the Bystander®. Both programs seek to involve communities and encourage cultural change—both steps in "baking it in."

According to their online promotions, Green Dot programming seeks change in institutional culture, stating their "ultimate goal" is to "shift community norms that support the violence that is occurring" (n.d., para. 3). Similarly, Bringing in the Bystander® advertises that their training "uses a community of responsibility approach" (2019, para. 1). Other than the webpages that promote their products, Green Dot and Bringing in the Bystander® exist behind proprietary walls.

Rather than use a proprietary, packaged program, some institutions have developed their own approaches. The Massachusetts Institute of Technology's institutionally based program appears to be one of the best and is freely available online. MIT's Active Bystander resources include nine links to extensive information from "Assessing Situations," to "Strategies," to an "Advice Column." Given its extensive resources and open access, MIT's resources are ideal for bystander training review before readers consider the scenarios in Chapter 4.

The most in-depth study of bystander training effectiveness was completed in England. Looking to implement bystander training in UK universities, Public Health England completed a "Review of Evidence" in 2016. The authors noted that most of the evidence included came from the United States in the years 2014–2015 (p. 5). It concluded that "Emerging evidence suggests that if implemented at scale, over time, bystander programming in university contexts can lead not only to positive attitudinal and behavioural [sic] change at the individual level, but also, to a reduction in perpetration and victimisation [sic] at the level of the whole community" (Fenton, Mott, McCartan & Rumney, p. 57).

The Active Bystander movement is not without detractors. In a scathing critique, Lauren Chief Elk, a Native American Women's advocate, and Shaadi

Devereaux, an advocate for trans women of color, argued, "In a culture of violence, both victim and intervening bystander have little support to rely on and are likely to be re-victimized after the original assault. In this light, bystander intervention appears less as a weapon in the fight against sexual assault and more like an evolved form of victim blaming. Minimizing the difficult work of challenging the institutions that support violence, it shifts the responsibility of ending violence to those most vulnerable to it" (2014, para. 8).

Interactive Scenario Training

The authors of this book believe that the use of scenarios that can be analyzed and discussed is particularly appropriate for those in writing studies since much writing studies pedagogy is based on rhetorical approaches to problem-solving. Findings in the *National Academy Report* strongly support the kind of training that can take place using the Scenarios in Chapter 4. Those findings concluded that positive effects of sexual harassment training are more likely when it

- lasted more than four hours,
- was conducted face to face,
- included active participation with other trainees on interdependent tasks,
- was customized for the audience, and
- was conducted by a supervisor or an external expert (Johnson et al., p. 152).

The scenarios also provide the "customized training" that Victoria Lipnic, a co-chair of the EEOC's Select Task Force on the Study of Harassment, has encouraged. Rather than having employees sit through "a boring and impersonal online training session," she promotes training that is "live, in-person and customized to your workplace" (Foltz, 2016, para. 13). More about the use of scenarios in sexual harassment prevention training can be found in the introduction to Chapter 4.

Concluding this chapter by making sweeping claims is tempting. The desire to provide a "fix it" recipe to eliminate sexual harassment is strong, but eliminating sexual harassment is not a quick-fix situation because the problem is so deeply embedded in our culture. Cultural change happens slowly as Steve Denning (2011), a senior contributor at *Forbes* pointed out. An organization's culture, he argued, is "an interlocking set of goals, roles, processes, values, communications practices, attitudes and assumptions" (para. 1). None of these elements stand free of the others, but "fit together as a mutually reinforcing system and combine to prevent any attempt to change it" (para. 2). Although Denning was writing about change in the business world, transformation in the academic world functions similarly.

But change is possible, and writing studies is fertile ground for the cultural changes needed. Elaine Maimon pointed to her work as a writing program administrator as the place where she learned how to lead (14). Working on the "periphery" gave Maimon, "a crash course in developing focus, peripheral vision, and strategic thinking" (16) all of which are needed to promote cultural change. The rhetorical background of many in writing studies can also be instructive as vigorous moves to eliminate sexual harassment are put into place. A rhetor sensitive to *kairos*, "takes into account the contingencies of a given place and time, and considers the opportunities within this specific context for words to be effective and appropriate to that moment" (*Kairos*, para. 1). Taking these contingencies into account needs to be carefully considered, but not necessarily slow. The work of Eric Charles White (1987) is especially helpful when employing *kairos*. The word, he explained, means "the right moment" or "the opportune" and in archery, he continued, *kairos* refers to an opening or a "long tunnel-like aperture through which the archer's arrow has to pass" (p. 13). This requires that the arrow be fired both accurately and with enough power for it to breach the target. The *kairotic* moment has arrived for change in cultural attitudes and behaviors on sexual harassment. The time is right to "bake it in."

Chapter 4: Talking About It

Aaron Barlow
NEW YORK CITY COLLEGE OF TECHNOLOGY

Darsie Bowden
DePAUL UNIVERSITY

Kefaya Diab
INDIANA UNIVERSITY

William Duffy
UNIVERSITY OF MEMPHIS

Patricia Freitag Ericsson
WASHINGTON STATE UNIVERSITY

Whitney Myers
TEXAS WESLEYAN UNIVERSITY

Dianna Winslow
CALIFORNIA POLYTECHNIC STATE UNIVERSITY

Mark Shealy
TENNESSEE TECH UNIVERSITY

Kathleen Blake Yancey
FLORIDA STATE UNIVERSITY

The general Introduction to this book details its genesis, but the particulars of producing this chapter are noteworthy. As an initial step, participants interested in writing scenarios emailed me[1] and indicated the gist of each scenario they would like to write. The authors' backgrounds ranged from graduate students to full professors, and some authors wrote more than one scenario.

Once a list of contributors was solidified, I provided general advice to all authors, emphasizing that the purpose of the scenarios was not *exposé* or titillation. On the contrary, the purpose was to offer snapshots of a range of experiences that academics might encounter. Another important goal in composing the scenarios was to keep all authors anonymous so that no scenario could be tied/traced to any individual or institution. Interestingly, as I read the scenarios, I

---

1. The introduction to this chapter was written by Patricia Freitag Ericsson, thus the use of first person pronouns in the first few pages.

DOI: https://doi.org/10.37514/PRA-B.2020.0988.2.04

found that bits and pieces of most of them (and a few of them in total) echoed my experiences in 35 years of higher education, which included working at a small university in the Great Plains, a technical university in the upper Midwest, and a land grant institution in the West.

The specific details I provided to the authors:

- a limitation on the maximum word count: approximately 1000 words and 4–5 discussion questions;
- a suggestion to look at the CCCC scenarios (http://cccc.ncte.org/cccc/committees/7cs/tenurepromotioncases) as well as the 2009 case study book (Maybe I Should . . .) by Hamrick and Benjamin;
- a caution that each scenario must be built from a patchwork of harassment possibilities, not drawn directly from any one author's individual experience;
- an additional caution that to protect each author's identity, names of people and institutions should be carefully masked.

I received the completed scenario drafts and checked each one for any identifying information which, if included, was deleted. Once all scenarios were uploaded to a Google Doc, all authors were invited to offer revision and editing advice. This part of the process was not anonymous; names of those offering advice were available to all authors.

Once the scenario drafts were revised and edited, the original authors were asked to revise and to once again email the revised scenarios to me. As in the previous iteration, the revised drafts were uploaded to a new Google Docs file. Final revisions were made by me and by three volunteers from among the scenario authors.

To support our goal of keeping authors anonymous, attribution for contributions to this chapter is not individual, but collective. Because of the collaborative process that was used, this attribution is indeed appropriate—beyond the necessity of privacy in dealing with a topic as fragile as this one. The psychic impact of drafting, reviewing, revising, and final editing of these scenarios was shared by all authors, not just individuals in the group.

As explained more fully in Chapter 3, the most effective way to prevent sexual harassment is to "bake" prevention into institutional culture. Typical sexual harassment training has little effect other than preventing institutions from liability. The 2018 *National Academy of Science Study, Sexual Harassment of Women Climate, Culture and Consequences* concluded that positive effects of sexual harassment training are more likely when it

- lasted more than four hours,
- was conducted face to face,
- included active participation with other trainees on interdependent tasks,
- was customized for the audience, and

- was conducted by a supervisor or external expert (Johnson, P. et al, p. 152).

This conclusion solidified our belief that the scenarios could be effective training materials.

Each scenario includes at least four discussion questions; consideration of these questions is strongly encouraged. Employing definitions from Chapter 2 can augment discussion of these scenarios. Use of each reader's or group of readers' institutional guidelines should unquestionably play a role in analysis as it relates to individual campuses.

Depending on readers' backgrounds, a multitude of theoretical lenses could also be used for improving analysis. Classical to Feminist Rhetorical Theory, Articulation Theory, Actor-Network Theory, Cultural and Gender Studies, Critical Race Theory, and more could be steps toward valuable insights. While analysis via personal experience should not be undervalued, particularly in analysis of emotionally laden incidents such as those in these scenarios, discussants are encouraged to augment the personal with other kinds of analysis.

Above all, and no matter which questions, definitions, or theories are employed in analyzing the scenarios, considering issues of power is vital. In fact, a strong argument could be made that all issues of sexual harassment are issues of power dynamics. Although most who read this book have likely considered or studied power relationships, a brief review of previous scholarship on power and sexual harassment is worthwhile.

In their 1984 book, titillatingly titled *The Lecherous Professor*, Billie Wright Dziech and Linda Weiner briefly discussed "powerlessness" and contend that "Women recognize early that power and sexuality are equated by society" (p. 82) and noted that student victims fear reprisals if they report sexual harassment. "Victims often believe that the authority of the professor equals power over their futures—in a sense, their lives" (p. 83).

Just a few years later, contributors to Michele Paludi's 1990 edited collection *Ivory Power* scrutinized (not surprisingly, given the book's title) power relationships. Kathryn Quina claimed, "The sexual harasser uses his age and social position, or wields economic power and authority as his weapons . . ." (p. 94). Vita Rabinowitz argued, "it is easy for students and professors alike to underestimate the power a professor possesses in his interactions with his students" (p. 104). And Darlene DeFour reached back to research from French and Raven's 1959 publication to understand categories of power: "(a) reward power, (b) coercive power, (c) referent power, (d) legitimate power, (e) expert power, and (f) informational power" (p. 46).

In 2006, Patrice Buzzanell and Kristen Lucas identified three gendered career dimensions: time, space, and identity. "The linear temporal orientation by which individuals classify and evaluate themselves and others has differential effects on the lives of women and men" (p. 166). Time in rank in the academic world can create a hierarchy in which women are disadvantaged, especially in experiencing and reporting sexual harassment. Space is an issue because "individual movements and locations connote power" (p. 167). The authors noted that a neutral workplace can be changed into an intimidating one by a male "telling profane jokes or making sexual references to or advances on women" (p. 169). Identity, they wrote, has many facets, but has been discussed as the way in which "individuals form their understanding of themselves in relation to their work over time and how these identities shift as individuals face particular career and/or life changes" (p. 170). Titles and rank identifiers are important identity markers in academia. Such markers leave many with lower identity labels more susceptible to harassment. Thus, time, space, and identity are all dimensions that impact power relationships.

Fast-forwarding to 2016, Ellen Mayock's *Gender Shrapnel in the Academic Workplace* does not directly name power, but it is an undercurrent throughout the text. Early in the book, Mayock argued "the gender norms of our homes and of our public interactions that consistently follow a patriarchal flow are replicated and entrenched in the workplace" (p. 6). Although not explicitly articulating it, Mayock's assertion rests upon an understanding of patriarchal power. In explaining gender shrapnel, she analogized it to "a series of small explosions in the workplace that affect women and men and reveal an uneven gender dynamic at all levels of the organization" (p. 6). Explosions are power-full, no matter if they are small. Mayock's "explosions" are grown in what Caroline Fredrickson (2017) called the "fertile territory" of academia. "Academia is particularly fertile territory for those who want to leverage their power to gain sexual favors or inflict sexual violence on vulnerable individuals" (para. 5).

Analysis and discussion of the scenarios that follow will not and cannot be easy and painless. Some scenarios may trigger difficult memories and reopen wounds. Care in dealing with readers' responses is, therefore, absolutely necessary. The voices of the many, not the powerful few, must be evoked and heard if the scenarios are to serve their purpose—that of learning and creating cultural change that will make writing studies a more equitable landscape—a landscape that is not fertile territory for leveraging power, but one that is rich ground for cultivating fairness and an equipoise of power.

Scenarios

Scenario 1: Writing Center Leadership

This scenario details a situation that may occur when tutors in a writing center are tasked with leadership responsibilities for which they may be unprepared or undertrained.

James is in his fourth year as the writing center director at University X. He is in a tenure-track position, but not yet tenured. After he was hired, one of the first projects he pursued was the development of a tutor professionalization initiative that paired more experienced tutors with newly hired and less experienced ones.

James asks "mentor" tutors to observe the sessions of "mentee" tutors twice per semester. In addition, mentor tutors are encouraged to occasionally reach out to their mentees to inquire about questions, concerns, or challenges they have regarding not only their work as tutors, but also how they are managing the labor of balancing writing center work with their other responsibilities as graduate students. For the past two years, James has assigned two mentee consultants to each mentor consultant. The program has been working well, until now.

Following a staff meeting with the writing center tutors, James is approached by a first-year Ph.D. student named Andrea. Having waited for her colleagues to leave the room, she discloses to James that another writing consultant, Rick, has been making her feel uncomfortable. She emphasizes to James that she, in her words, "doesn't want to get anyone in trouble," but explains that Rick will often greet her with a hug or sometimes walk with her, uninvited, to the class she has on Tuesday afternoons after her tutoring shift. She explains she is self-conscious about how this behavior looks; specifically, she is concerned that other tutors will think that she and Rick have a personal relationship beyond their work together in the writing center.

What makes the situation even more challenging is that Rick, a third-year Ph.D. student, is Andrea's mentor tutor. He is also ten years older than Andrea. Not only is Rick studying writing centers for his dissertation, he has been selected to serve as the writing center's assistant coordinator for the upcoming academic year, a one-year position awarded to advanced graduate students interested in developing their experience as a writing center administrator.

During her conversation with James, Andrea insists that she doesn't want him to approach Rick about his behavior. She just wants James to be aware of it because she is planning to confront Rick herself if this behavior persists. She does, however, ask if she can forego participating in any mentor/mentee-related activities. James tells Andrea that because there are less than two months left in the academic year, the mentorship program is all but completed and that there is no need for her to interact with Rick in a mentee-mentor context. Furthermore, James asks Andrea if she would like her regular tutoring shifts to be rescheduled so that there is no overlap between her work schedule and Rick's. She declines this invitation, saying the situation "is not that bad." Andrea thanks James and asks him to keep their conversation about this matter confidential.

Two weeks later, Andrea visits James during his office hours. She is nearly in tears. After James asks Andrea if she is okay, she tells him that Rick just confronted her in front of the other tutors. She explains that after her initial discussion with James about Rick's behavior, she started to dodge Rick whenever they were both working. On this day, however, Rick approached Andrea in between two of her sessions and asked if everything was okay because she has been "acting weird." He also asked her if he had done anything wrong. Apparently, several days earlier Rick sent Andrea an email requesting that they meet for coffee to discuss her first year as a writing consultant. She did not respond to this request.

After he approached her in the writing center, Andrea told Rick that everything was fine and that she just had a lot of work to do. According to Andrea, Rick then asked when they could get coffee. Feeling even more uncomfortable, Andrea told Rick that she didn't want to get to coffee and that she needed to get back to work. At this, Andrea says, Rick "lost it" and proceeded to lecture her about how if she wanted to be a successful writing consultant she needed to take her work more seriously. At this point, all activity in the writing center came to a temporary standstill. Andrea then asked another consultant if they could cover her next scheduled appointment and immediately came to James's office.

Unsure how to proceed, James thanks Andrea for coming to speak to him, expresses his sympathy that she must cope with Rick's behavior, and tells her that he needs to consult with his own supervisors. For the time being, he says, she does not have to work her scheduled writing center hours when Rick is also scheduled. Even though James has a tenure-track appointment in English, the writing center is funded through Academic Affairs. While the Assistant Provost for Academic Affairs signs off on the writing center's budget, she otherwise does not exert any administrative oversight of the writing center's day to day business, nor does the English department. For these reasons, James is unsure who exactly to contact about this matter.

Discussion Questions

1. Should James take into consideration the gender dynamics of mentor-mentee pairings?
2. During their first conversation, Andrea asks James to keep this discussion confidential. Even if Andrea did not report activity that on its face is recognizable as harassment—especially when Andrea herself does not identify this activity as such—what options does James have?
3. In this scenario, the writing center exists in a liminal position relative to the university's bureaucracy. Its director has a tenure-track position in English, but the funding for the center comes through Academic Affairs. How should James proceed? What college/university policies or procedures might exist to help navigate this scenario?
4. Depending on how this situation gets resolved, what are some strategies for moving forward, especially if Andrea and/or Rick continue as writing tutors? How should James discuss this matter with other writing center staff, if at all?

Scenario 2: International Student-Teacher/Advisor

This scenario considers the possible complications that might arise when an international graduate student requires employment to stay in the country and is uncomfortable with the professor she is working for.

Putre is an Indonesian graduate student at X university, holding an F1 student visa and working as a TA in her department. Starting her third semester she focuses on her thesis research with the intent to apply to Ph.D. programs after graduation. To maintain lawful residency in the U.S, Putre plans on obtaining an Optional Practical work visa (OPT). This visa allows Putre to work for a full year after graduation as a research assistant to her advisor, Dr. John Smith, while waiting for her Ph.D. program to begin.

However, for the past year, Putre has started feeling that Dr. Smith's friendly gestures toward her don't seem quite right. Putre and Dr. Smith frequently work in his office, usually sitting around a small table with their laptops open. Putre feels he pulls his seat or leans his head too close to hers when discussing something related to their research or looking at her computer screen. She tries to avoid these situations by moving her computer closer to his side to allow him a clearer view, but he always manages to push the computer back towards Putre and pull himself closer to her again. Sometimes Putre can smell his breath and cologne and often, Dr. Smith complements the smell of her perfume and hair products. This makes her so uncomfortable that she stops using perfume purposefully every time she has a meeting scheduled with him.

Although Putre feels uncomfortable, she is not sure if Dr. Smith's behavior is harassment, and she suspects he is blind to her discomfort. Putre admires Dr. Smith highly for his intelligence, guidance and support, and she believes she is growing as a scholar because of his mentorship. Putre suspects that her discomfort stems from cultural differences: perhaps Americans are not as private and conservative as Indonesians? However, Putre does not consider herself to be too conservative, and she has other male faculty members, colleagues, and friends who communicate with her closely, giving her hugs on occasions without causing her any discomfort. For some reason, Putre feels guilty and embarrassed by the whole situation. On one hand, she might be making a problem out of nothing, and on the other, she might inadvertently be giving Dr. Smith the green light by not saying anything about how his behavior makes her feel.

At this point, the situation is starting to cause Putre a significant amount of anxiety. Dr. Smith is the only professor in her department who really seems to understand and care about her research. He was the only one to have offered her a temporary job after graduation. If she was to tell him she is not comfortable with the way he physically gets close to her, he might feel offended, change the way he treats her as an advisor, move her to another faculty advisor, or most importantly, withdraw his research assistant job offer to distance himself. However, the other option sounds as bad to Putre: if she does nothing, the situation might remain the same or even get worse over time. Putre considers ignoring the whole situation to focus on her master's degree. She wishes to graduate without further complications, hoping that she will have a better chance to figure things out after that.

Discussion Questions

1. As a colleague or friend of Putre's, what advice would you give her? How might your own clusters of beliefs, experiences, and values influence the way you respond?
2. Putre feels limited in how she might address her working situation. If she chooses to share her concerns with Smith, what might happen to her, to Smith, to other students and faculty, to the department, and to the university as a whole? Conversely, if Putre chooses to remain silent, what might happen to her, to Smith, to other students and faculty, to the department and to the university as a whole?
3. If a student's legal residence is dependent upon employment, what resources, training, and existing community should be available for students, staff, and faculty to help anticipate, address, and facilitate healthy working relationships between international students and the professors/programs they work for?
4. How do differences in culture complicate already challenging power dynamics between students and professors? What resources are available at your institution that help address and facilitate healthy working relationships between international students and the professors/programs they work for?

Scenario 3: The Chair Retires?

This scenario details what might occur when an accused aggressor has retired but harassment still continues as a result of the aggressor's remaining relationships with faculty and staff.

The chair was retiring. His protégé had recently been promoted to a level where she could replace him. The last hires he had been responsible for were now finishing their first year successfully. One of them, a young Latina scholar, Julia Gonzales, had broken away from the chair's mentorship (without explaining why to anyone). She had, nonetheless, been given a new contract. The election for a new chair was uneventful, and the outgoing chair graciously promised to be around to give advice.

In February the following year, Julia approached Henry Garratt, the one young and untenured member of the Appointments Committee. Other than Henry, the Appointments Committee was dominated by the old guard of the department. Julia told Henry she was worried about her annual review, even though it was to be conducted by the new chair. Julia said she knew that, at the behest of the past chair, the new chair was "out to get her." Henry asked why. She explained that she had refused the old chair's advances. This experience had led Julia to refuse further contact with the old chair. He had tried to make her feel as though she "owed" him and they, according to her, had bitter parting words.

Henry promised to keep an eye on things, but he said there was very little he could do if Julia was not willing to bring a grievance—something she felt she might not be able to do given that the aggressor had retired. Neither Julia nor Henry was sure, so Julia decided not to pursue the question.

Julia's second annual review was quite critical. Julia's third-year contract was issued, but she was worried that she would be denied a fourth-year contract based on a review whose negativity, she felt, stemmed from the influence of the past chair.

The most senior member of the Appointments Committee, Joanna Stetson, had been a close colleague of the retired chair for more than twenty years and was now serving as senior advisor to the new chair. Joanna volunteered to observe Julia and write a teaching review; the report was scathing. That, along with Julia's poor annual review, made the likelihood of a new contract remote. Julia asked for a second observation, which the chair herself completed. It, too, was negative.

Alarmed, Julia began telling others about the situation, always tracing it back to the retired chair and always adding that she thought there might be a racial element as well. She continued to refuse, however, to initiate any action, feeling it was pointless and dangerous, for it was the old chair's friends who were now harassing her in his stead. Once again, Julia spoke to Henry and to her dean, who told her he could do nothing more than watch the situation and make sure that all required protocols were adhered to. He told her that she could write rebuttals for her file in all three instances but Julia declined to do so.

The following year, when it came time for the department's Appointment Committee to make its renewal recommendations to the college Personnel and Budget Committee, almost everyone in the department was aware of the situation because Julia had spoken openly about it. In the meeting, Henry was trying to argue the case for Julia when a knock came on the door of the conference room. It was Julia, who wanted to present her own case. Such a thing was unheard of; no protocol was in place that allowed for candidates up for renewal to plead their case. She was told no and was asked to leave the area, which she did not do. The Committee ended the meeting and decided to reconvene at a later day.

The Appointment Committee's vote was not to be made public; the report only went to the Promotion & Budget Committee where it would not be announced to the public either. Julia eventually received a non-renewal letter, a decision that could only be appealed directly to the university president. Julia appealed the decision.

Discussion Questions

1. Henry, the young professor on the Committee, decided to meet privately with the president, apprising her of the situation. When the non-renewal was eventually appealed, the president overruled it, allowing Julia to remain in the institution's employ. Was Henry's visit to the president

appropriate give the situation's history? What kind of disclosure responsibility, if any, does Henry have to his colleagues and/or to Julia?

2. When someone, as a result of perceived harassment, is unable (for whatever reason) to act rationally in their own defense, should another step in—even if having no direct knowledge of the truth of the harassment charge?

3. At which points in the scenario could Julia chosen to take other actions? What actions could she have taken? What may have prevented her from doing so?

4. What are the limits to what one can do for a colleague?

Scenario 4: Faculty/Staff Dynamics

This scenario considers the dynamics between department faculty and staff, especially when it comes to socializing outside of work.

Jennifer was recently hired by the Department of Writing and Rhetoric at XYZ University as the new administrative support specialist for undergraduate studies. In addition to managing adjunct contracts, serving as an assistant to the director of first-year writing, and maintaining syllabi and other records for the department's general education courses, she also moderates the department's social media feeds and assists with various PR initiatives on an ad hoc basis. Three weeks into this new position, Howard Smith, a tenured professor in the department, invites Jennifer out for drinks with other department faculty and staff. Jennifer heard that these outings, which usually occur on Fridays, are a fairly common and informal affair. She told Howard yes. When Jennifer arrived at the bar where these gatherings typically occur, Howard was there with a group of seven other department faculty and staff members.

The following week Howard again dropped by Jennifer's office to invite her out for drinks. Even though it was a Thursday—Jennifer assumed everyone only went out on Fridays—she had a good time last week getting to know some of her colleagues, so she again told Howard that, yes, she'd like to attend. Around 4:45 that afternoon, Howard dropped back by Jennifer's office and invited her to walk with him to the bar.

When they arrived at the bar, however, Jennifer didn't see anyone else from the department. Furthermore, and much to Jennifer's surprise, Howard asked the greeter for a table for two. At this point, Jennifer felt uncomfortable. While she had a good time with everyone the previous week, Howard had made this sound like another informal departmental gathering when in fact this meeting was more like a date. But Jennifer was unsure how to interpret what Howard had done. Did he "ask her out" in the romantic sense? Or was this just his way of trying to be friendly? The ensuing conversation was pleasant enough—Jennifer kept their talk focused on work-related topics—but after 30 minutes she told Howard she had a previously scheduled engagement and needed to leave.

Over the next three weeks, Howard didn't ask Jennifer out for drinks again, but he occasionally dropped by her office for an informal conversation. While these conversations haven't made her uncomfortable, they sometimes lasted upwards of fifteen or twenty minutes and thus were a distraction that prevented Jennifer from doing her work. Sometimes he would even sit down without Jennifer inviting him to do so. Jennifer had considered keeping her office door closed, especially when she knows Howard is in the hall, but this would be tricky because technically she needs to be available for faculty and other staff members who need her assistance. Then, three days ago Howard stopped by her office and started to initiate another conversation when Jennifer was working, but this time she politely told him that she couldn't chat because she needed to finish some work.

Jennifer did not see Howard for the next two days, but the following day, when she got to the office, she found a book in her mail cubby with a note on it from Howard. It asked Jennifer to make copies of several chapters from the book and to leave them in his mailbox. In the note, he thanked her for this "favor." While part of Jennifer's job does involve assisting professors with course preparation, no part of her job involves serving as a personal assistant for faculty. Jennifer was unsure how to proceed. She didn't want to comply with Howard's request, especially since she didn't want to give him the impression that this work falls under her normal job duties. Yet she was unsure how best to respond to Howard. Should she ignore the request? Should she inform him that he needs to make his own copies? Should she ask the department chair how to proceed?

Discussion Questions

1. It can be common in some academic workplaces for faculty and staff to socialize at restaurants or bars at the end of a workday. If you organize one of these informal meetings, what are strategies for ensuring that such invitations aren't coercive, especially for those who don't occupy similar positions in the academic bureaucracy?

2. What options are available if someone finds themselves in a position like Jennifer does when she realizes Howard has asked her out on an apparent date? What about when someone might pursue frequent, informal interactions that are uninvited, just as Howard does when he drops by Jennifer's office to chat?

3. Can and should non-official department socializing, especially when it involves organizing during the workday using university resources (such as the school's email domain) be subject to university or department-initiated rules and regulations?

4. How can departments ensure that its staff, especially staff like Jennifer who have well-defined responsibilities, are not mistreated by faculty whose interactions with them may or may not on the surface be influenced by gender bias?

Scenario 5: Grad Student and Mentor

This scenario details the possible complexities that can arise between Ph.D. students and their dissertation chairs.

Mary applies to the Ph.D. program at University X primarily because David Smith, an emerging scholar in her field, teaches there. He contacts her, expressing interest in her writing sample and indicating he has received approval for funding a research assistant next term. While visiting campus, Mary has coffee with Dr. Smith where they discuss funding possibilities, the classes he is teaching next semester, and her past graduate work. Only eight years older than Mary, the two quickly establish an easygoing relationship: he tells her to call him "David," drives her around town pointing out neighborhoods where students frequently live, and provides a list of local restaurants and bookstores. Mary accepts a position as an incoming student and research assistant; she leaves campus feeling as if she has found an important mentor in David.

During Mary's first few years at the university, she serves as David's research assistant. They co-author two articles, and he becomes her dissertation chair. She becomes involved in a professional organization in which he serves as a member of the Advisory Board. Occasionally, Mary runs into him at a pub across from the university. During these informal conversations, David seems more like a friend, sharing pedagogical struggles, successes, and failures.

While their relationship is relatively easy, occasionally Mary is aware of its gendered dynamics. Prior to a conference presentation, David casually mentions that they should probably discuss the clothes Mary will wear as she begins to interview. "After all," he says, "You don't want the length of your skirt giving anyone the wrong impression." Mary simultaneously regrets the height of the heels she is wearing and is annoyed that David feels it is appropriate to comment on her appearance.

One night, Mary and her boyfriend run into David and his wife at a restaurant. Shaking her boyfriend's hand, David compliments him on his "good taste" and jokes that he hopes her boyfriend won't "take too much of Mary's time away from her research." Another time, David asks Mary details about her new relationship. Slinging an arm around her shoulders, he says, "Don't let him distract you from what's important." While his comment makes Mary uncomfortable, she also understands that because of the time he has put into mentoring her, David wants to ensure she completes her degree successfully.

Mary has now completed a draft of her dissertation and spends extensive time with David discussing revision strategies. One evening before leaving his office, David grabs her arms and abruptly kisses her. Mary pushes him away, shocked at the gesture and angered by his impropriety. David rushes to apologize, saying it has been a long week and things are rough at home. The next day, he sends her a text that simply says, "Please keep last night's mistake to yourself. It could ruin both of our careers." Mary agrees. Any professional blowback to David's reputation adversely affects Mary, especially as he begins to write letters of recommendation to Mary's potential employers.

However, Mary becomes increasingly frustrated. David misses two of their scheduled meetings and is spending more time working with his first-semester research assistant. Later, three sources central to Mary's research are missing from his office; David says he has not seen them in weeks. During a committee meeting, David abruptly cuts Mary off while she is talking and after, huddles in the corner with the newly appointed department chair. They both look over towards her, multiple times. An article of David's which Mary has contributed to via her work as a research assistant appears in a journal; unlike earlier drafts, Mary's contribution is neither identified nor cited. Finally, David indicates he needs more time writing Mary's letter of recommendation for her job portfolio; he feels her work in the last semester has suffered from distractions "outside" of the department. Mary is furious. While many of the previous incidents created disruption to her schedule or could be written off as mere coincidences, some feel intentional and, more importantly, have direct professional repercussions.

Talking to a friend, Mary cautiously outlines the "professional" problems she is experiencing with David to a friend, making certain not to mention his more recent, frequent patterns of "harmless" behavior. The friend mentions that prior to Mary's arrival, David had experienced similar issues with a graduate student that left the program. However, she says, that was a different situation—she had heard the graduate student was inappropriately pursuing a relationship with David that he curtailed. Carefully, she suggests that Mary might be overreacting or misinterpreting the situation. "Are you sure you're not taking this too personally?" she asks.

Mary considers talking to the department chair, but the graduate handbook does not provide a channel for such a conversation. Conversation with other students reveals a departmental pattern of ignoring student/faculty relationships as long as they are perceived as "mutual." Moreover, there doesn't seem to be a network within the university to track student/instructor complaints regarding personal behavior. Instead, it appears that if and when students experience problems with these relationships, the student leaves the program and is constructed in department lore as "problematic," "emotional," and "retaliatory." Mary is worried how the pursuit of any claims about appropriateness of behavior will affect the completion of her degree and future employment opportunities.

Discussion Questions

1. How does your position as a graduate student, faculty, or member of the administration shape the way you read and respond to Mary's story?
2. What would you identify as the troublesome or concerning characteristics of Mary and David's mentor/mentee relationship? How would you

describe a healthy mentor/mentee relationship between a junior faculty member and graduate student?

3. In what ways do Ph.D. programs encourage potentially problematic relationships between students and faculty members? What options and resources should be available for students and faculty when potential problems arise?

4. What are the practical options available to Mary as a student nearing the completion of a terminal degree?

Scenario 6: Cultural Questions

How much should cultural background be used to excuse what we might otherwise recognize as inappropriate behavior? While every situation is different, it can sometimes seem as though mitigating circumstances are nothing more than excuses. This scenario considers such issues.

Dean Angelo Garguilio, born in Italy, had been living in the United States for fifteen years when he was appointed to his position. He had been teaching at the university since he joined the institution, at fifty, to take an endowed chair, invited because of his renowned scholarship and international reputation. He was happily married, or so it seemed, and had grown children. He presided over the College of Liberal Arts, where most of the chairs, at the time, happened to be women. He was succeeding a female dean who had been promoted to provost.

Garguilio was respected but not loved. In fact, he was not an easy man even to like. Not only was his accent difficult for many Americans to understand, but he was also overly personal, especially with female colleagues—something generally passed over by his superiors as a result of his own cultural background, i.e., as something that had to be understood and worked around. When he was promoted to dean, he had been chair of his department for five years. Members of the department couldn't decide whether to be relieved or concerned at this advancement.

As dean, Garguilio took over leadership of a particularly fractious group of chairs, some of whom he wanted to see removed. He couldn't do this himself, but he hoped to show his support to various opposition groups within the departments. The chairs saw this and those who felt threatened retaliated by working to remove *him*. Chief among them was, coincidentally, another Italian, a woman, who chaired the Comparative Literature department. From an outside perspective, in their machinations against each other, neither side acted particularly honorably—though neither side would have understood how or where the problems lay.

Despite his leadership role, the dean had never been a supervisor of any sort before becoming chair, and his own department had been a small one. The three women who worked in his office quickly came to dislike him. Though he never made sexual advances toward them, they felt he looked down on them not only for not having advanced degrees but also because they were women. He was demanding and supercilious, immune to the difficulties they encountered in their work and unsupportive of their own needs and desires.

Among the chairs, he was little more liked, having developed comfortable relations only with the two males of the eight in total. The other six, the women (including the person who had replaced him in his own department), fell victim to snide comments and brusque dismissals. They retaliated by trying to undercut him through the provost, who all of the chairs knew well.

Complained to by individual chairs, the provost talked to the dean on a number of occasions about his treatment of women. He should not, she advised, comment on clothing or give even a friendly kiss. Certainly, a lingering touch should be avoided and he should never tell a woman colleague that she was looking particularly sexy. And he should listen when women spoke, not fidgeting as though anxious to move on. Clearly perplexed, he promised to change his ways, but he never managed to do so. He didn't seem to understand just how his behavior was objectionable. Knowing that he had never acted in a sexually predatory manner, he never managed to grasp exactly what the problem was.

After two years of what was, quite obviously to some, sexist behavior, the female chairs had had enough. They got together and filed Title IX charges against the dean for creating an atmosphere of sexism that impeded the growth and activities of the chairs. The investigation, handled by a university lawyer, was quite flawed, its putative secrecy abrogated at every step. Eventually, the president and provost, recognizing they might lose the case but realizing the dean needed to be removed, negotiated a leave for the dean necessitating his leaving his post. On return, he found himself effectively exiled from his own department, even his office moved from the building that housed it to a site on the opposite end of the campus, the new chair not wanting to have what she saw as an unruly and threatening presence return to the department.

Could it be that this dean lacked the cultural understanding necessary for serving in an administrative position in a U.S. university? He had absolutely no understanding of what he had done and felt that the women had ganged up against him. He felt he had treated the chairs equally, men and women, and that his choices for friendship had nothing to do with gender. Though he did not lose his job, he felt the ignominy of the events and knew that what was meant to have been secret was not. Instead of ending his career on a high note, he retired as quickly as he could.

Discussion Questions

1. In multicultural environments like those of higher education institutions, what kind of resources should be available for students, staff, and faculty to become culturally sensitive in their communications and actions?
2. How does one's position in a university culture oblige them to call out culturally insensitive or inappropriate behavior?
3. Could there be alternative avenues other than removing the dean?

4. Specifically, is there an effective place somewhere between ignoring behavior and initiating a Title IX investigation?

Scenario 7: Online Sexual Harassment

This scenario concerns an online composition class taught by an experienced female, full-time, non-tenure-track instructor and a student whose troubling behavior crosses several lines.

On the first day of class, Leah (a 34-year old female instructor) posted two general announcements on her class's learning management system: one was about class policies, and the other was about the first assignment, which was a 300-word introductory statement intended as an icebreaker. Peer responses to introductions were required. On day five of class, Farrell (a 24-year-old male student) posted what Leah described as "overly friendly" comments to the introductory statements by three female students. After sending Farrell a private message in which she asked him to refrain from posting such messages, Leah saw that he had posted a 200-word statement in the informal "lounge" section of the online class remarking how the instructor was probably a "cat lady" in need of a man for sex.

Leah was shocked and upset over this personal attack, which contained some obscene language. Farrell followed up his initial posts with additional ones containing what was later described by Leah as "overtly sexual and threatening comments on how he wanted to force himself sexually on female students." Farrell later claimed he intended the language to be "funny" rather than threatening. Leah deleted two of Farrell's posts before deciding to document the incident and sent an email to the department chair, Sarah, who was new to the position. Leah then emailed all students in her online classes, attaching an English department document that included general institutional guidelines for student behavior, to remind them of college policy regarding bullying and sexual harassment.

On day seven of class, Instructor Leah and Department Chair Sarah filled out an incident report, which was sent to Student Affairs and the dean's office. They also discussed how to confront Farrell. Leah believed that the situation was immediately dangerous; Sarah thought care should be taken to acknowledge student rights for both the women and Farrell. While debating whether to remove Farrell from class, Leah and Sarah could not agree about how online harassment situations differed from threats on campus and how or if an online student might be a "physical danger." Leah sent Farrell an email, cc'd to Sarah, about his inappropriate postings and attached a copy of college policy regarding general harassment. Leah and Sarah searched online for information about Farrell, although they wondered if they were breaking some sort of ethical code by trying to investigate Farrell's digital presence.

On day eight, Leah and Sarah found pictures on Farrell's Instagram and Twitter accounts showing him smoking what appeared to be marijuana and pointing what appeared to be a real gun at the camera. Both women began to worry about possible physical violence. Five female students emailed Leah to say that they would not be attending an on-campus class orientation scheduled for the next week out of fear that Farrell would attend. Sarah suggested that Leah not cancel the orientation since security would be checking the classroom. Leah received a vaguely apologetic email from Farrell in which he claimed he was "just messing around" when he posted the comments. Department Chair Sarah emailed Farrell and instructed him to meet with a college counselor, Jonathan. Leah sent screen captures of the disturbing social media images to Jonathan to illustrate what she considered "violent potential" in Farrell.

Orientation took place on campus at 6:00 PM on day nine of class. Two members of campus security were present—but Farrell did not attend. Sarah discovered that Farrell worked for the college part-time in the Student Recreation Center. The fact that Farrell had access to staff areas on campus alarmed Leah, Sarah, and Jonathan. However, the dean, Richard, seemed less disturbed. The dean emailed Sarah indicating that he wanted the issue to be dealt with as quickly—and quietly—as possible.

On day eleven of class, Jonathan and the dean's office informed Sarah that Farrell was not being fired from his job on campus, adding that he had been told by a male supervisor to "cut out the behavior." Leah emailed the women who were concerned about his threats and encouraged them to remain in class. Farrell dropped the class. Department Chair Sarah asked Leah to sign additional documents sent by Campus Security, legal counsel with Student Affairs, the dean's office, and Jonathan.

A month later, Leah heard through the grapevine that Farrell was never fired from his job at the college, but he chose to quit for reasons seemingly unrelated to this incident. She was also told that Farrell claimed to some students and staff members that he had been treated unfairly by Leah because he was the only male African-American student in the class. Emotions among all involved had subsided, but Department Chair Sarah told Leah that she worried many legal and ethical lines might have been crossed in handling the matter.

Discussion Questions

1. What assumptions about sexual harassment, online education, and institutional policies do you bring to your reading of this narrative?
2. How might we account for the Department Chair Sarah's reaction to these events in relation to the Instructor Leah's? To what extent are both Sarah and Leah concerned for the same things? How would you react if you were in either Sarah's or Leah's position?
3. Although the fact is not disclosed until the end of the narrative, how might racial identity play a role in how Leah and Sarah viewed the situation as opposed to how Farrell viewed it? Might Farrell, as the only African-American man in the class, have a legitimate point about being judged unfairly?

4. How is online sexual harassment in this narrative presented as a problem distinct from on-campus harassment? How might institutional policies that address sexual harassment need to differentiate between what happens in digital environments and what happens on campus?

Scenario 8: Graduate Student Instructors and Their Students

This scenario explores issues that develop between female graduate student instructors and male students at a large, private university.

University X's program for graduate students in composition and rhetoric is competitive and provides a range of opportunities for supervised teaching in the university's first-year composition program. Graduate students who are accepted attend a pre-term, three-day workshop that provides detailed information on the FYC program and preparation of classroom activities, assignments, and response strategies. These new instructors follow an annotated syllabus designed by the supervising faculty member for the first half of the term, after which they can craft their own classroom activities and assignments. As instructors teach their first course, they also take a companion graduate teaching practicum that provides week-to-week guidance and problem-solving.

Recently, students in both the graduate program and the teaching apprenticeship have been predominantly female. In the current term, six graduate instructors in the teaching program were females and two were male, all between the ages of 22 and 30. Most had also taken the writing center training course and were involved in writing center work. Several had previous teaching experience although not in first-year composition, and some had presented at local and national conferences. They were knowledgeable, confident, and predictably excited and nervous about the upcoming teaching experience.

Part of each class period in the practicum was set aside for debriefing on the week's teaching—successes, challenges, and questions. The first two weeks of the term went reasonably well, with predictable missteps and bumps as the new instructors familiarized themselves with the workload and the challenges of juggling classroom prep and responding to student work. Instructors testified to how pleased they were with how their students reacted to them.

Beginning the third week of classes, a worrisome trend began to emerge and eventually dominated discussion. The female instructors reported on disconcerting exchanges with some of their male students. While the incidents varied in nature, by the end of the term nearly all the female graduate instructors reported troubling interactions with male students. The two male graduate instructors listened attentively and were very supportive to their female colleagues, but they reported none of the seemingly gender-based conflicts.

One of these graduate instructors, Lucy, described a series of incidents with one of her male students that "made her uncomfortable." The student, an eager classroom participant, regularly stayed after class to talk about the course. Eventually, his talking points became more personal as he pressed her about her tastes in music, food, and movies. One day, the student came up to her in the university cafeteria and gave her a big hug. When this unwanted physical contact happened again, the instructor realized she had to do something. She asked the student to meet with her, and, as gently and firmly as she could, explained that while she was flattered, his behavior was inappropriate and would have to stop. The student seemed stunned, but he indicated that he understood and apologized. From that moment on, however, the student refused to participate in class, began missing classes, and was inconsistent about turning in work. The instructor spoke to him again, encouraging him to keep up, explaining that he could do well in the class, but his classroom work continued to deteriorate.

Another graduate instructor, Mia, organized a computer-classroom workshop in which students could work on their in-progress essays. The instructor circulated around the classroom providing help and suggestions as they worked. One male student seemed to be working on an essay that did not follow the instructions for the assignment. Mia talked to him about it and made suggestions. He nodded, then continued to work. As Mia came around to him again, he was still moving in the wrong direction, so she spoke to him again. This time, he seemed very irritated by her intrusion. At the end of the class, students submitted their essays electronically to their portfolio site for instructor response and evaluation. When the instructor read this particular student's essay, she was stunned. The essay had turned into an angry, sarcastic diatribe in which he expressed his desire to either smash her in the face if she continued to give him advice, or better yet, pull out a gun and shoot her.

Late in the term, Elise, another graduate instructor, admitted to ongoing problems with a student in her class—a male student, a few years older than the rest of the first-year students. The student, perhaps sensing that she was a new instructor, would yell at her angrily during class if he thought an assignment was pointless or felt like she wasn't being clear enough. Despite her private one-on-one interventions with him outside of class, this belittling behavior, often in the form of loud outbursts, continued throughout the term both inside and outside of class.

These and other incidents were shared in the practicum and discussed by the graduate instructors and the supervising faculty member to develop strategies for handling them. In most cases, the graduate instructor was encouraged to contact the Academic Affairs office to solicit advice and recommendations on how to proceed. The response from the university was less than optimal. Although the young man with ideas about pulling a gun on his instructor was taken seriously (though not expelled), the other investigations led to quick fixes. Instructors were asked to ignore the problems and see if they went away on their own. The instructors, all of whom were young and new to the profession, were uncomfortable about these solutions, but obliged.

Discussion Questions

1. How familiar are you with your own institution's policies and resources available on harassment? To what extent do these policies and resources advocate for female instructors in particular?

2. Recent articles in the media (for example, "Chief Targets of Student Incivility Are Female and Young Professors" in *The Chronicle of Higher Education*) suggest a trend in the kinds of issues discussed in this scenario. How does this scenario align with your experiences?

3. One component of the training these graduate instructors received was work on creating a teaching persona. As a final project for the companion course, the graduate students wrote a reflective piece about the evolution of their teaching persona—their perceived successes and challenges. How might you address the creation of a teaching persona in anticipation of the problems above?

4. Several of the instructors were quite angry that they were experiencing these kinds of problems, assuming it does not happen to male instructors. How true does this seem to be in your experience? What are the challenges of having to prepare young female instructors for this type of harassment and how should male instructors be trained in this regard?

Scenario 9: Student-Student-Student

Are problems in relations between graduate students things that should be addressed by members of the department?

William is a new MA student and a TA in the English department in a midsized top-tier research school in a conservative town. He identifies as gay and he has just broken up with his boyfriend. William feels lonely and insecure in this new town, starting an MA program, and teaching for the first time in his life. He lives on campus in the graduate student apartments and is hoping to engage in campus life, avoiding contact with the local community. When William meets Rayan, a second-year Ph.D. student, he starts having hope that the two would develop a friendship and an academic partnership.

Rayan has been a TA since he joined the department. The department considers Rayan a star scholar and teacher. Not only does he thrive in his research and with his undergraduate students, but he has also accumulated impressive experience in community-based research and service focused on sexuality as social justice. Rayan has a wide circle of friends around the university and in the town. He identifies publicly as straight, and he has a girlfriend, Jade, who moved with him when he relocated.

Over time William, Rayan and Jade develop a close friendship. As they live off-campus and own a car, Rayan and Jade always offer rides to William. William is grateful and feels lucky to have been accepted intellectually and socially by this couple.

Spending considerable time at Rayan and Jade's apartment, the three cook, talk, and watch movies. Although attracted to Rayan and somewhat jealous of his happy relation with Jade, William feels included; he wishes he could find a happy relationship like theirs someday.

When William starts noticing Rayan coming in close physical contact with him while sitting on the couch or cooking at the kitchen, William isn't sure whether this happens intentionally. The physical contact triggers William's emotions, but he doesn't act upon them to avoid complicating his friendship with the couple and his interactions with Rayan in the department. William also considers that the physical closeness was probably unintentional.

However, things change suddenly in a way that William has not anticipated. One evening Jade and Rayan pick William up from his on-campus apartment and take him to theirs where they cook and have dinner as usual. As they are having their second drink, Rayan and Jade join William on the living room couch, putting him in the middle, which feels weird to William. Rayan asks William whether he would like his palm to be read, and Jade chimes in that Rayan is good at it. William feels he has to say yes and he opens his hand for Rayan, who starts moving his fingers on William's palm, reading his past and future. William feels that the touching and Rayan's tone of voice are undoubtedly sexual.

William stays passive and lets Rayan finish his reading though everything feels weird and confusing. He is aware of his vulnerable situation, one person versus two. He is at their apartment off-campus, and he does not have any means of transportation other than their car. He feels he needs to be friendly with the couple until he is able to leave. He tries to make a joke out of the situation, saying, "You guys feel weird tonight. Are you too drunk?!"

Eventually, Rayan leaves the couch, mentioning that he has work to finish; Jade offers William a ride home. During the ride, William tries to fill the silence by complementing Rayan's and Jade's relationship in an attempt to assert himself as a friend who is not interested in a romantic relationship with the couple. Jade, however, tells him clearly that they have lots of love to give, and that he is welcome to join them. This comment makes William feel very uncomfortable. Dropping William off, Jade turns her cheek to him to kiss. Like a robot, William gives her that kiss, regretting it and hating himself.

Once in his apartment, William texts both Jade and Rayan saying that he really appreciates their friendship but is going to stay away for a while. Jade responds by apologizing that she and Rayan had scared him off and assured him they appreciate his friendship as well. That night William can't fall asleep. He feels mixed feelings of guilt, fear, and shock about what happened. He was uncertain whether he did or said something that gave Jade and Rayan the wrong impression.

Trying to put an end to his uncertainty, and fearing the loss of friendship with the couple, William texts both Rayan and Jade first thing in the morning asking them to meet and clear things up. William hopes to restore the friendship. Rayan responds inviting William to the couple's place, but William asks to meet in a public place. He then receives a confrontational text message from Rayan blaming him for his distrust in asking for a public meeting. Rayan becomes defensive and aggressive and reminds William of all the good things that he and Jade have done to make William feel loved and at home.

William, totally crushed, feels at a total loss, experiencing embarrassment, guilt and fear. He feels disappointed, weak and sexually abused. He immediately goes to the campus counseling center seeking help and relief.

Discussion Questions

1. What type of power structure can allow a situation like this to develop?
2. If you were a professor or chair in the department, what kind of advice would you have for William and Rayan?
3. How might the incident affect William overall? How might it affect his study, work, and interaction in the department?
4. If you were a friend of William's and he came to you for advice, what would you have said? Why? What does this tell about you? How might that advice conflict with William's values, thoughts, and experience?

Scenario 10: Can Age and Experience Excuse Behavior?

This scenario details the challenges a professor experiences during her first year as a tenure-track hire at a small liberal arts university.

As a newly minted Ph.D. in rhetoric and composition, Alina is a 32-year old recent hire teaching a 4/4 load in the English department at a small liberal arts school. She is the first English hire in eight years; while friendly, her colleagues are all significantly older. Alina is newly pregnant, and her partner works at a university three hours away.

Settling into the semester and her role as faculty member, Alina is surprised how different a small college is from the larger universities she attended. She meets faculty from a number of different departments, all of whom are friendly and enthusiastic about her hire. At a reception for new faculty, the chair of the biology department, Dr. Roberts, who also serves as the faculty senate chair, speaks to her individually and remarks that she looks "really young," suggesting that some students might struggle with someone who "looks like her" in charge of the classroom.

"How old are you anyway?" he queries. Taken aback by the question, Alina doesn't want to rock the boat with a senior colleague she barely knows and reassures him she has quite a bit of experience teaching. In retrospect, Alina is frustrated by her behavior; she wishes she had been clear about the offensiveness of his comments and resolves to speak up if a similar situation presents itself again.

The following semester, Alina is responsible for describing the development of a writing emphasis within the English major to the larger faculty body. This is a project she is passionate about; she is nervous about her presentation and, at first, glad to see a familiar face in the room: Dr. Roberts. Eyeing her up and down he exclaims, "Well, well . . . look who has a bun in the oven! Congratulations!" Giving her a hug, he says, "I didn't see a ring so figured you were one of those feminists!" Alina is irritated and expresses her feeling, yet Dr. Roberts dismisses her discomfort. Walking away to call the meeting to order, he remarks to a female colleague standing nearby, "These new hires are all so sensitive." Stunned, Alina stares at the faculty member, who laughs and places a hand on Alina's arm. Leaning in, she says, "Don't take Dr. Roberts seriously. He's been here a long time and doesn't mean any harm."

When it is her time to present the departmental changes, Alina reads from a statement she has prepared. She is highly aware of her shaky voice and slight roundness of her pregnant body, along with her anger towards Dr. Roberts and the female colleague who defended him. Halfway through her presentation, Dr. Roberts interrupts: "Basically," he says, "It sounds like our new professor wants students to take a less traditional approach to their English degree and focus on that new media stuff the university is so fond of." Alina starts to object and again, Dr. Roberts speaks over her. "Why don't you just send the description to me, and I'll forward it to the faculty?" Alina looks around the table for some support but most of the faculty are looking down at phones or appear uninterested. Alina slowly sits down.

A few weeks later, Dr. Roberts asks Alina to meet with him to discuss the proposal. Alina dresses carefully for the meeting, making sure to avoid any clothing that emphasizes her pregnancy. Dr. Roberts closes the door to his office after she enters and invites her to sit down. When she remarks that she would feel more comfortable with an open door, Dr. Roberts ignores her. He tells her he's heard students in his lab classes complaining about her writing course for being "too hard" and has suggested to them her expectations are simply "hormonal." As faculty chair, he wants to know if she's happy at the college.

Next, he slides over to her side of the desk, placing the folder containing the department proposal open on her legs. Leaning over, he points to various concerns he has. There is nowhere for Alina to move; she panics at his proximity, his breath, and his overly comfortable manner.

When done with his questions, Dr. Roberts places his hand on top of the folder. "I just think you need to have a little fun," he says. "Why don't we go have dinner and talk more about your ideas?" Alina firmly removes his hand and clearly states, "Your behavior makes me uncomfortable and is distinctly inappropriate. I'd appreciate our relationship remaining professional." She walks out the door.

Although concerned about being labeled a troublemaker, Alina goes directly to her department chair to discuss the meeting with Dr. Roberts. A tenured female professor who has been at the university for twenty years, her department chair listens carefully to Alina's complaints about Dr. Roberts: his focus on her appearance, her pregnancy, his behavior towards her at the faculty meeting, his inappropriate remarks about her teaching to his students. While sympathetic, her chair suggests that Alina simply should avoid interacting with him if she finds his behavior offensive. The chair then observes that filing a grievance against a tenured faculty member is complicated and has rarely been used, noting that Dr. Roberts has been an esteemed member of the university community for the last 30 years. She points out that Alina is only in her first year of a tenure-track position and isn't yet a very strong presence on campus beyond teaching and required meetings. "Instead of attending campus events, I've been focused on publishing pieces of my dissertation," Alina says. "Yes," her chair agrees, "yet very few people on campus know you well enough to vouch for your 'collegiality' because of this."

Alina walks away from their meeting upset and embarrassed. She feels as if her concerns were dismissed and her collegiality and understanding of tenure responsibilities called into question. Left wondering if she has simply overreacted to the inappropriate, old-fashioned behaviors of a longstanding faculty member, Alina sees no pathway to a formal complaint or support for her concerns.

Discussion Questions

1. How would you proceed as the department chair? As Alina?
2. How do differences in institutional size pose challenging questions/complications regarding faculty behavior, relationship, and formal complaints?
3. Alina has addressed the problematic behavior with the individual involved and her department chair. What other resources should she pursue?
4. How do age, gender, institutional, and faculty history complicate this situation?

Scenario 11: WPA and Assistant Mentoring

This scenario describes how a white, heterosexual cisgender female WPA took advantage of perceived intimacy with the male Assistant WPA and used it politically to smooth over the fallout from her behavior and control the story of her labor, accomplishments, and merits.

Leo Foster had known Karen Johnstone through academic and friendship circles several years before he started working with her. Leo had come to his associate WPA position through a network of acquaintances that included Karen, as often happens in the field of Rhetoric and Composition. This was his first permanent job in the field. Leo was grateful not to be a freeway flyer, whisking himself and his materials to adjunct jobs at multiple institutions. He felt deep gratitude that he had a little edge because of friends of friends who knew him and his work.

All of this was evident in the opening moves of this new employer/employee relationship, and it provided a platform for important mentor-mentee interactions. Leo expected to be mentored, and he did not notice, or was naïve about, the ways Karen used familiarity and perceived close connection to quickly build intimacy. At this beginning stage, casting it as an "honor," Karen used this premature intimacy to vent her frustrations about WPA work, the low program budget, and the lack of respect she perceived from College of Liberal Arts colleagues.

She tried to shape Leo's impressions of colleagues, mapping for him her intended political maneuvering to "get back at" those who were keeping her from the material resources she wanted for the program, or to "demand" the professional respect she felt was "overdue." Leo did not know what to do with much of this information.

Nor did Leo know that he would become the target of her anger and frustration as their work relationship progressed, eliciting it simply by offering a different interpretation of an encounter or scenario.

Though Leo gained confidence and knowledge over time, there was no accompanying and appropriate transfer of power and responsibility; Karen had no place for a colleague, he began to see, merely for an unquestioning subordinate. As Leo developed authentic opinions of and relationships with their common colleagues, Karen withdrew her confidences. Transparency became an issue, and Leo was often left out of the loop on important decisions affecting his areas of work. When he raised the issue of transparency, he was told that it was his imagination, that she had been open, and why wouldn't she be, with someone she trusted so implicitly? Didn't Leo trust she was making the right decisions for "us"?

When projects Leo led were appropriated as her work, and he said something, he was told that it was a team effort, and she was simply presenting material to the higher levels of the university's administration to which she had access but he didn't. Even though she could have made the introductions necessary for him to present his own work, she did not.

When Leo began to build and train a strong writing instruction team, Karen began selecting and removing key players from the team, tapping them to do other work without consulting them or Leo. All along the way, she explained away unilateral decisions by telling him to trust her; they were good friends, remember? She surely wouldn't take credit for work that wasn't hers. And yet she did.

None of this seemed quite right to Leo, but it also didn't seem quite wrong enough for action. He was in the first few years of his first full-time job; he wasn't even sure if he knew how this was supposed to go. Leo had been trained by principled and honest WPAs in his graduate program and had spent much of his graduate career thinking and writing about power dynamics and privilege in classed and ranked systems.

The more Leo drew on that training and developed his own collaborative and transparent leadership style for the projects he supervised, the more at odds he and Karen became. This led to her shaming Leo in public meetings, dismissing his comments and contributions. Later, Karen would ask him to excuse her rudeness, saying that it was just that they were such good friends, like family, and don't we all argue with our family?

At some point during this time, Karen's husband Jake (who was faculty in Sociology and had befriended Leo from the outset) invited Leo to have a beer after work. Leo sat in disbelief as Jake explained earnestly, "Karen really does have your best interests in mind." It was then, three and a half years in, that Leo realized he was in what amounted to a codependent, abusive relationship with his direct supervisor. Now her husband was involved.

Leo didn't know how to extract himself from this unwanted power struggle without endangering his position. He thought he could finally see what was wrong, but didn't know how to fix it, nor did he know where to go for help or whom to trust for guidance.

Discussion Questions

1. How can "common sense" ideas about workplace power dynamics affect the perceptions and behaviors of new employees?
2. How can institutional and cultural norms provide the underlying foundation/support/justification for the described scenario?
3. How can (forced) intimacy in a professional setting affect power dynamics between two people of unequal rank, regardless of the gender identity or sexual orientation of the people involved?
4. Do new employees in your institution receive information about how to address sexual harassment, discrimination, or assault in the workplace?

Scenario 12: Graduate Faculty and Graduate Student

This narrative begins with a graduate class taught by Julie, a tenured Rhetoric/Composition faculty member at a research institution, and her interactions with a doctoral student, Walter.

After class one evening during the spring term, Julie, a tenured professor in rhetoric and composition, walked to her office accompanied by Walter, a first-year doctoral student. Excited by the class conversation on visual rhetoric, Walter asked if they could keep talking, and Julie, ready to go home after a long day, said, "Of course, as long as you walk with me to my office."

"Great," Walter replied, as he returned to the question of how common it was for images to change as they moved through contexts—and how important that might be for a theory of circulation.

At the office, Julie packed up her things while Walter kept spinning out examples of images; they walked away from her office, down the hall, and out of the building toward the parking lot. The evening was pleasantly cool but, as was common at that time of night, very few students were around. Interrupting his queries about images, Walter paused, asking, "It's ok if I keep walking with you?"

Julie replied, "Sure, but I'm almost at the car."

She began to add, "I'm glad to meet with you later in the week if you'd like to keep talking," but Walter interrupted: "I'll walk you to the car."

Julie, thinking that Walter was being protective, asserted, "No, really, it's ok," but Walter kept walking; two minutes later, they were at the Honda. Pushing her electronic key, she opened the back door and tossed in her backpack, closed the door, and turned around, only to find Walter bending over her and pushing himself up against her. "I think a kiss would be nice, don't you?"

Taken aback, Julie exclaimed, "What are you doing, Walter?"

"Just helping us get closer: you asked me to walk with you to your office," he breathed softly, as he tried to kiss her neck.

"Walter, no, no, that was only because," she started to explain, when Walter said, "Don't tease me; I know you want this as much as I do."

"NO!! Julie yelled; "I don't."

Momentarily chastened, Walter stepped back: "Ok, Julie," he replied, "you're right; we're in public. We'll do this another time," he said quietly but intently, as he turned away and quickly strode back toward the building.

Shaken, Julie slipped into her car, simultaneously slamming the door and locking it. She wasn't quite certain what had happened, and she couldn't quite believe that whatever it was *had* happened. Walter had seemed like such an interested student.

No student had ever approached her in this way, not in 15 years of teaching. Should she tell anyone about this? Whom would she tell? What would she want them to know?

Julie didn't sleep well that night. She worried that somehow she had signaled to Walter that she was interested in a physical relationship with him, and she worried about what to do about that. She worried about if and how to follow up with him. Should she ignore this episode and treat it as an anomaly? Should she speak to him to correct his misunderstanding? She worried about whether she should alert others about this: Was he behaving this way toward other faculty or students? Should she tell her department chair about this episode? Or, wary about all of these discussions, should she simply ignore the episode? That last option, ignoring it, was the easiest and most familiar, to be sure, but in this case, was it the best response?

Julie saw Walter the next week in class; he behaved as though nothing had happened, which was a relief; perhaps doing nothing was the best response. When he left the room at the end of class, though, Julie thought she saw Walter winking at her.

Or was that her imagination?

Julie continued trying to return to acting normal. With only three weeks left in the term, she thought she might just succeed. As usual, she scheduled the conferences that she required students have with her before submitting their final projects. Although she didn't want to meet with Walter, she didn't see how to avoid it, but she took care to schedule all of the conferences during busy times of the day, and as usual, she would keep her door open.

The conferences had proceeded normally when Walter arrived for his. They had a brief discussion about his project, which wasn't very well designed, with Julie making three suggestions toward a major revision. Walter seemed unhappy about the need to do a considerable amount of additional work, but he indicated that he knew what it was and why. As he got up from his chair, he seemed to take on another persona: winking at her, he said softly, "I think about our special moment a lot." Julie, standing up, replied, "Walter, you need to go now."

"Of course," Walter responded. "See you soon."

Julie picked up the phone to call her chair, asking if she were available for a quick consultation. "Come on up," the chair said. Breathless, Julie collapsed in the chair's office as she begins her story: "I have a problem with a student, Walter Smith."

"Oh, that cute young grad student in your program? He is such a good student—and a fine teacher, I hear."

"Yes," replied Julie, wondering if this consultation with her chair would provide a remedy after all.

Discussion Questions

1. Has Julie experienced sexual harassment? How, specifically? Are there mitigating factors (e.g., gender, age, status)?
2. What evidence can Julie present to demonstrate that something untoward has happened? How could that affect her decision about pursuing the issue?
3. After the first episode, what options did Julie have? Julie identifies some; are there others, and if so, what are their advantages and disadvantages? What repercussions might each have?
4. As a colleague or chair who was approached by Julie for advice, what recommendation would you make after the first episode, and why? After the second episode?

Scenario 13: Graduate Seminar and Gender

The challenges of seminar topics and gender are explored in this scenario.

Mary Morris, a new faculty member in the rhetoric and composition program at Big Bend State University (BBSU), was teaching her first graduate class, "The Rhetorics of Gender and Sexuality." Because she was new and had written her very recent dissertation in this area, students were initially excited to take her course. A few weeks into the semester, however, several students were upset.

Because of Mary's recent arrival, her reading list and syllabus were not available until the first day of class. On the first day, students were surprised that most of the readings were about male power and privilege, toxic masculinity, and rape culture. In a private conversation after the first class, three of the five male students in the twelve-person seminar voiced their concerns to each other about the readings but decided that considering the rhetorical aspects of these topics would be worthwhile.

By Week 5, the initial concerns of the three male students were becoming more serious. In further outside-class conversation, they found their worries were shared by the other male students as well as two female students. Instead of an even-handed rhetorical approach to the topics, the seminar had become a venue for telling stories of sexual abuse and for damning particular cultures for encouraging and producing "macho-male" attitudes and predatory behaviors. The representations put forward in class made the men in the class (two African American, one Latino, and two white men) feel unfairly represented and occasionally attacked. When they spoke up in class, they were regularly shut down, and the teacher did not intervene. The two women who attempted to allow the men a voice in the class were verbally sidelined by the others. After one particularly contentious class session, one of the two women distressed by the attitude toward men was warned by another female student that by siding with the men she was "a traitor to her gender."

The seven concerned students talked and decided to send an emissary to the teacher. Two of the male grad students set up an appointment, and Mary greeted them cordially. As they voiced their concerns, Mary nodded, but eventually told them there was nothing she could do to change the tenor of the seminar. She explained that she was not willing to intervene because she was a strong believer in a student-led pedagogy even though it might create controversy and chasms. When the two male students told her they felt bullied and sometimes harassed in the class, she smiled and simply said, "Well, that's turning the tables, isn't it?"

The male grad students left Mary's office with a sense of disbelief. When they told the others about the interaction, all seven became upset and confused. They needed the seminar credits, but they wondered if they could continue in the class. The two who visited Mary's office were worried that their grades would be compromised by the interaction. All of them wondered what, if anything, they could do.

Discussion Questions

1. Is there bullying, discrimination, or harassment taking place in this seminar? What BBSU documents could be consulted to answer this question?
2. Should the students report this situation? How might a complaint to the department chair or Human Resources be received?
3. Could creating waves possibly harm their careers? In what ways?
4. What assumptions about learning, faculty rights, student rights, and more seem to be in play in this scenario? Given those assumptions, what is the appropriate course of action for each person concerned?

Scenario 14: Bystander Responsibility

This scenario considers how involved a bystander should be, especially in a case in which the bystander knows the possible aggressor.

Jana, a student in the Rhetoric and Writing Studies graduate program at X University, works several times a week in the writing center (WC). The WC is staffed by graduate and undergraduate tutors and supervised by a director and assistant director. Now in her second year as a tutor in the WC, Jana is familiar with consultation protocol and the best practices that the director and assistant director review in their monthly training sessions.

Jana has noticed that Tom, a tutor who is also a graduate student in the program (in fact, Jana and Tom are members of the same cohort), has been flirting with several female undergraduate students who have come to the WC for consultations. This is not unlike his behavior with members of their cohort, Jana wryly noted to herself the first time she observed it. In fact, Tom had flirted heavily with Jana their first year, and she finally needed to firmly reject him. She had done so as gently as she could and, as far as she could tell, had hidden her distaste for Tom well. She knew that she needed to keep a collegial relationship with him. They both were still in coursework, so Jana didn't want to create a scenario that would make working alongside Tom in the program any more difficult than it already had become. Since then, Jana and Tom's relationship had been somewhat distant although they had no trouble working together in the WC. Jana had never since spoken to Tom directly about his WC behavior and had avoided socializing with him.

But, in addition to the overt flirting, Jana had recently overheard Tom make questionable comments and suggestions to the female undergraduate students, comments that go beyond the bounds, she is pretty certain, of appropriate tutor/student relations. Jana had heard Tom ask them about their class schedules, for example, and what they like to do on the weekends for "fun." At least twice, Jana had heard Tom offer "extra help" to these women if they want to contact him after hours when the WC is closed. This disturbs Jana, but she does nothing at first, worried that she is reacting to her own distaste for Tom, overreacting to what she worries might or might not be unwarranted advances. She knows that Tom is going well beyond flirting—and she recognizes that flirting itself is something of a problem in this context.

The assistant director comes in and out of the WC office space (her office is located on the floor above the WC) and Jana has come to realize that Tom has never engaged in this questionable behavior when the AD is present. In fact, most of these incidents occur during a two-hour window on Tuesday afternoons when Jana, Tom, and one undergraduate tutor, a junior named Emily, are the only tutors on shift.

Jana is concerned about Tom's behavior, but doesn't know what to do, especially given her own feelings concerning Tom. Is she, she asks herself, worrying about something that is none of her business simply because of her own distaste for Tom? Also, she suspects that the AD is aware of what had happened between the two of them and guesses that she might even have them working some of the same hours so that she provides balance to Tom.

Given her own reluctance to face Tom about this new manifestation of his behavior, she hasn't asked Emily about it, although Jana is curious if she has noticed anything. Also, Emily is an undergraduate, so Jana doesn't want to put her in an awkward situation where she may have to speak out against this more-senior graduate student coworker.

Discussion Questions

1. To keep from making waves, Jana is considering talking to some of her fellow grad student friends about this situation. Is this a good approach? Why or why not?

2. What additional evidence, if any, does Jana need to report this situation as sexual harassment?

3. If Jana does report the behavior, to whom should she turn? She knows both the director and assistant director, but she has a much closer relationship with her advisor in the graduate program, so she is considering talking to her. Is this a good idea?

4. What kinds of policies or protocols might the director (and assistant director) of a WC put in place to help bystanders like Jana when they witness behavior like Tom's? What about if bystanders witness behavior that isn't so explicit? That is, what if Tom wasn't visibly flirting with these students, but still offered them "extra help" during times when the WC is closed? Is that still grounds for concern?

Chapter 5: Learning More About It

Mark Shealy

TENNESSEE TECH UNIVERSITY

This bibliography contains a diverse selection of articles, books, chapters, and professional and/or governmental publications that covers literature in English related to sexual harassment, sexual assault, and discrimination in regard to writing studies. While the list touches on issues of intersectionality in terms of gender, race, class, language, ethnicity, religion, etc., the main focus remains on documents whose central subject is sexual harassment, sexual assault, or sexual discrimination. The terminus ad quo is 1964, beginning with the Civil Rights Movement, and ends in 2018. Because the topics of sexual harassment, sexual assault, and discrimination are so extensive and covered in depth across a range of academic literatures, this bibliography is meant to serve as a starting point for the researcher. Included here are useful search terms with which to begin a database search. This list is drawn from most common search terms based on Library of Congress subject headings, the Google AdWords Keyword Tool, and Wordtracker.com.

- Rape kits
- Rape trauma syndrome
- Sexual assault definition
- Sexual assault statistics
- Sexual assault statute of limitations
- Sex discrimination against women
- Sex discrimination in employment
- Sex discrimination in higher education
- Sexual harassment definition
- Sexual harassment hostile environment
- Sexual harassment in education
- Sexual harassment in the workplace
- Sexual harassment in universities and colleges
- Sexual harassment investigation
- Sexual harassment law and legislation
- Sexual harassment of women
- Sexual harassment of men
- Sexual harassment policy
- Sexual harassment prevention
- Sexual harassment quid pro quo

DOI: https://doi.org/10.37514/PRA-B.2020.0988.2.05

Articles

American Association of University Professors. (2009). Statement on professional ethics. In *AAUP Reports & Publications*. https://www.aaup.org/report/statement-professional-ethics.

American Association of University Professors. (2014). Sexual Harassment: Suggested policy and procedures for handling complaints. In *AAUP Reports & Publications*. https://www.aaup.org/report/sexual-harassment-suggested-policy-and-procedures-handling-complaints.

Angelone, D., Mitchell, D. & Carola, T. (2009). Tolerance of sexual harassment: A laboratory paradigm. *Archives of Sexual Behavior, 38,* 949–958.

Anon, 2015. Sexism at the centre: Locating the problem of sexual harassment. *new formations: a journal of culture/theory/politics, 86*(1), 34–53.

Bagley, C., Natarajan, P., Vayzman, L., Wexler, L. & McCarthy, S. (2012, March/April). Implementing Yale's sexual misconduct policy: The process of institutional change. *Change,* 7–12.

Bay, J. (1999). Who's afraid of their male students?: Voicing discourses of authority, resistance, and harassment in the composition classroom. *Dialogue: A Journal for Writing Specialists, 5*(1), 31–45.

Bergman, E. & Henning, J. (2008). Sex and ethnicity as moderators in the sexual harassment phenomenon. *Journal of Occupational Health Psychology, 13* (2), 152–167.

Biber, J., Doverspike, D., Baznik, B., Cober, M. & Ritter, B. (2002). Sexual harassment in online communications: Effects of gender and discourse medium. *Cyberpsychology, Behavior, and Social Networking, 5*(1), 33–42.

Biemiller, L. (2010). "I saw him making out with a dude." *Chronicle of Higher Education, 57*(7), A3.

Bingham, Shereen G. & Burleson, Brant R. (1996). The development of a sexual harassment proclivity scale: Construct validation and relationship to communication competence. *Communication Quarterly, 44*(3), 308–325.

Block, J. (2012). "Prompt and Equitable" explained. *College Student Affairs Journal, 30*(2), 61–71.

Bondestam, F. (2004). Signing up for the status quo? Semiological analyses of sexual harassment in higher education-A Swedish example. *Higher Education in Europe, 29*(1), 133–145.

Bradley, G. (2016). Sexual harassment guidelines. *Academe, 97*(6), 4.

Britt, M. & Timmerman, M., (2013). Penn State University, Title IX, Clery Act and sexual harassment: Was the old boy network at work? *Journal of Applied Management and Entrepreneurship, 18*(4), 64–78.

Buchanan, N. T., Bergman, M. E., Bruce, T. A., Woods, K. C. & Lichty, L. L. (2009). Unique and joint effects of sexual and racial harassment on college students' well-being. *Basic & Applied Social Psychology, 31*(3), 267–285.

Bursik, K. & Gefter, J. (2011). Still stable after all these years: Perceptions of sexual harassment in academic contexts. *Journal of Social Psychology, 151*(3), 331–349.

Calafell, B. (2014). Did it happen because of your race or sex?. *Frontiers: A Journal of Women Studies, 35*(3), 75–95.

Calder-Dawe, O. & Gavey, N. (2016). Making sense of everyday sexism: Young people and the gendered contours of sexism. *Women's Studies International Forum*, 55, 1–9.

Cargile Cook, K. (2000). Writers and their maps: The construction of a GAO report on sexual harassment. *Technical Communication Quarterly*, 9(1), 53–76.

Citron, D. (2009). Law's expressive value in combating cyber gender harassment. *Michigan Law Review*, 108(3), 373–415.

Davidson, M. M., Gervais, S. J. & Sherd, L. W. (2015). The ripple effects of stranger harassment on objectification of self and others. *Psychology of Women Quarterly*, 39(1), 53–66.

Dervin, D. (2011). 2010: The year of the bully. *Journal of Psychohistory*, 38(4), 337–345.

DeSouza, E. R. (2010). Frequency rates and correlates of contrapower harassment in higher education. *Journal of Interpersonal Violence*, 26(1), 158–188.

Dibble, J. (1993, Dec. 23). A rape in cyberspace: How an evil clown, a Haitian trickster spirit, two wizards, and a cast of dozens turned a database into a society. *The Village Voice*. http://www.villagevoice.com/news/a-rape-in-cyberspace-6401665.

Diehl, C., Glaser, T. & Bohner, G. (2014). Face the consequences: Learning about victim's suffering reduces sexual harassment myth acceptance and men's likelihood to sexually harass. *Aggressive Behavior*, 40, 489–503.

Diss, L. E. (2013). Whether you "like" it or not: The inclusion of social media evidence in sexual harassment cases and how courts can effectively control it. *Boston College Law Review*, 54(4), 1841–1880.

Downing, G. (2013). Virtual youth: Non-heterosexual young people's use of the internet to negotiate their identities and socio-sexual relations. *Children's Geographies*, 11(1), 44–58.

Ferrer-Perez V. & Bosch-Fiol, E. (2014). The perception of sexual harassment at university/La percepción del acoso sexual en el ámbito universitario. *International Journal of Social Psychology*, 29(3), 462–501.

Franks, M. A. (2012). Sexual harassment 2.0. *Maryland Law Review*, 71(3), 655–704.

Fusilier, M. & Penrod, C. (2015). University employee sexual harassment policies. *Employee Responsibilities and Rights Journal*, 27(1), 47–60.

Gardner, S. (2009). Coming out of the sexual harassment closet: One woman's story of politics and change in higher education. *NWSA Journal*, 21(2), 171–195.

Gelms, J. (2012). High-tech harassment: Employer liability under the title VII for employee social media misconduct. *Washington Law Review*, 87(1), 249–279.

Greff Schneider, R. (1987). Sexual harassment and higher education. *Texas Law Review*, 65, 1–60.

Grossman, J. (2015). Moving forward, looking back: A retrospective on sexual harassment law. *Boston University Law Review*, 95, 1029–1048.

Hall, R., Graham, R. & Hoover, G. (2004). Sexual harassment in higher education: a victim's remedies and a private university's liability. *Education & The Law*, 16(1), 33–45.

Hobson, C. & Szostek, J. (2015). The development of a content valid tool to assess organizational policies and practices concerning workplace sexual harassment. *The Industrial-Organizational Psychologist*, 52(4), 111–119.

Human Rights Campaign. (2014). Resources: Tyler Clementi higher education anti-harassment act, H.R. 482; S. 2164. http://www.hrc.org/resources/entry/tyler-clementi-higher-education-anti-harassment-act.

Jaleel, R. (2016). Beyond sexual violence. *Academe, 102*(3), 55.

Jaschik, Mollie L. & Fretz, Bruce R. (1991). Women's perceptions and labeling of sexual harassment. *Sex Roles: A Journal of Research, 25*(1–2), 9–23.

Jones, A. (1996). Desire, sexual harassment, and pedagogy in the university classroom. *Theory Into Practice, 35*(2), 102–109.

Joubert, P., Van Wyk, C. & Rothmann, S. (2011, Feb. 9). The effectiveness of sexual harassment policies and procedures at higher education institutions in South Africa. *SA Journal of Human Resource Management.* http://sajhrm.co.za/index.php/sajhrm/article/view/310.

Kelderman, E. (2008). Supreme Court to hear case that could limit sex-bias claims against colleges. *Chronicle of Higher Education, 55*(7), A19–A19.

Kelly, M. L. & Parsons, B. (2002). Journal of higher education: "Sexual harassment in the 1990s: A university-wide survey of female faculty, administrators, staff and students." *Women and Language, 25*(2), 548–568.

Kennedy, M. A. & Gorzalka, B. B. (2002). Asian and non-Asian attitudes toward rape, sexual harassment, and sexuality. *Sex Roles: A Journal of Research, 46,* 227–238.

Kimble, K. Farnum, K., Weiner, R., Allen, J., Nuss, G. & Gervais, S. (2016). Differences in the eyes of the beholders: The roles of subjective and objective judgments in sexual harassment claims. *Law and Human Behavior, 40*(3), 319–336.

Lampman, C., Phelps, A., Bancroft, S. & Beneke, M. (2009). Contrapower harassment in academia: A survey of faculty experience with student incivility, bullying, and sexual attention. *Sex Roles, 60*(5), 331–346.

LaRocca, M. A. & Kromrey, J. D. (1999). The perception of sexual harassment in higher education: Impact of gender and attractiveness. *Sex Roles, 40*(11–12), 921–940.

Legal Information Institute. 47 U.S. Code § 230—Protection for private blocking and screening of offensive material. http://www.law.cornell.edu/uscode/text/47/230 28.

MacKinnon, C. (2016). In their hands: Restoring institutional liability for sexual harassment in education. *The Yale Law Journal, 125,* 2038–2105.

Mansell, J., Moffit, D. M., Russ, A. C. & Thorpe, J. N. (2017). Sexual harassment training and reporting in athletic training students. *Athletic Training Education Journal, 12*(1), 3–9.

Mantilla, K. (2013). Gendertrolling: Misogyny adapts to new media. *Feminist Studies, 39*(2), 563–570.

Mansfield, K. C., Beck, A. G., Fung, K., Montiel, M. & Goldman, M. (2017). What constitutes sexual harassment and how should administrators handle it? *Journal of Cases in Educational Leadership, 20*(3), 37–55.

Marshall, C., Dalyot, K. & Galloway, S. (2014). Sexual harassment in higher education: Re-Framing the puzzle of its persistence. *Journal of Policy Practice, 13*(4), 276–299.

Megarry, J. (2014). Online incivility or sexual harassment? Conceptualising women's experiences in the digital age. *Women's Studies International Forum, 47,* 46–55.

Mitchell, K. M. W. (2017, June 15). It's a dangerous business, being a female professor. *The Chronicle of Higher Education (Advice section)*. http://www.chronicle.com /article/It-s-a-Dangerous-Business/240336/?cid=VTKF1.

Napolitano, J. (2015). "Only yes means yes": An essay on university policies regarding sexual violence and sexual assault. *Yale Law & Policy Review, 33*(2), 387–402.

Parker, I. (2012, Feb. 6). The story of a suicide. *The New Yorker*. http://www.new yorker.com/magazine/2012/02/06/the-story-of-a-suicide.

Penrod, C. & Fusilier, M. (2010–2011). Improving sexual harassment protections: An examination of the legal compliance of U.S. University sexual harassment policies. *Journal of Workplace Rights, 15*(2) 151–167.

Pew Research Center. (2014, Oct. 22). *Online Harassment*. http://www.pewinternet .org/2014/10/22/online-harassment/.

Phipps, A. & Young, I. (2015). Neoliberalisation and 'Lad Cultures' in higher education. *Sociology, 49*(2), 305–322.

Quinn, R. (1993). 'I should learn to see the truth as great men have seen it': Male mentoring, seduction, and sexual harassment in higher education. *Feminist Teacher, 7*(2), 20–25.

Rabelo, V. C., Cortina, L. M. & Bull Kovera, M. (2014). Two sides of the same coin: Gender harassment and heterosexist harassment in LGBQ work lives. *Law and Human Behavior, 38*(4), pp.378–391.

Ramson, A. (2006). Sexual harassment education on campus: Communication using media. *Community College Review, 33*(3/4), 38–54.

Ranney, F. (2000). Beyond Foucault: Toward a user-centered approach to sexual harassment policy. *Technical Communication Quarterly, 9*(1), 9–28.

Reports by M. Vohlidalova and co-researchers describe recent advances in higher education (Coping strategies for sexual harassment in higher education: "An official action may harm you in the end more than if someone slaps your butt"). (2015). *Science Letter, 99*.

Sexual harassment: A female counseling student's experience. (1991). *Journal of Counseling and Development, 69*(6), 502.

Shelton, J. N. & Chavous, T. M. (1999). Black and white college women's perceptions of sexual harassment. *Sex Roles: A Journal of Research, 40*(7–8), 593.

Smolović Jones, S., Boocock, K. & Underhill-Sem, Y. (2013). '[PDF] beingha-RasseD?' Accessing information about sexual harassment in New Zealand's universities. *Women's Studies Journal, 27*(1), 36–48.

Stein, N. (2007). Bullying, harassment and violence among students. *Radical Teacher, 80*, 30–35.

U. S. Department of Labor. (1972). *Title IX, education amendments of 1972 (Title 20 U.S.C. sections 1681–1688)*. https://www.dol.gov/oasam/regs/statutes/titleix.htm.

U. S. Equal Employment Opportunity Commission. (2014). *Laws, regulations & guidance, types of discrimination, sexual harassment*. http://www.eeoc.gov/laws /types/sexual_harassment.cfm.

U.S. Equal Employment Opportunity Commission. (2011). *Sexual harassment charges: EEOC & FEPAs combined: FY 1997–2011*. https://www.eeoc.gov/eeoc /statistics/enforcement/sexual_harassment.cfm.

Washington, F., Kahla, M. C. & Crocker, R. M. (2015). Sexual harassment on campus: "He's just a pervert and everybody knows it!". *Journal of the International Academy for Case Studies, 21*(6), 215–219.

Waterman, C. (2016). How many select committees does it take to change the government's mind?. *Education Journal, 272*, 14–15.

Weisbuch, M., Beal, D. & O'Neal, E. C. (1999). How masculine ought I be? Men's masculinity and aggression. *Sex Roles, 40*(7/8), 583–592.

Werder, C. Howard, R. M. (2000) Rhetorical agency: seeing the ethics of it all. *WPA, 24*(1–2), 7–26.

Whitley, L. & Page, T. (2015). Sexism at the centre: Locating the problem of sexual harassment. *New Formations, 86*, 34–53.

Whitley Jr, B. E. & Keith-Spiegel, P. (2001). Academic integrity as an institutional issue. *Ethics & Behavior, 11*(3), 325–342.

Wood, L., Hoefer, S., Kammer-Kerwick, M., Parra-Cardona, J. R. & Busch-Armendariz, N. (2018). Sexual harassment at institutions of higher education: Prevalence, risk, and extent. *Journal of Interpersonal Violence.* https://doi.org /10.1177/0886260518791228.

Wood, L., Sulley, C., Kammer-Kerwick, M., Follingstad, D. & Busch-Armendariz, N. (2017). Climate surveys: An inventory of understanding sexual assault and other crimes of interpersonal violence at institutions of higher education. *Violence Against Women, 23*(10), 1249–1267.

Monographs

Brownmiller, S. (1975). *Against our will: Men, women, and rape.* Simon & Schuster.

Brownmiller, S. (2013). *In our time: Memoir of a revolution.* Random House.

Clarke, H. (2012). *Sexual harassment in higher education: A feminist poststructuralist approach,* [Doctoral dissertation, University of Derby]. ProQuest Dissertations & Theses Global (U606837).

Cornell, D. (1995). *The imaginary domain: Abortion, pornography, and sexual harassment.* Routledge.

Crutcher, C. & Hartwell-Hunnicutt, Kay. (1996). *Sexual harassment in higher education: The male perspective* [Doctoral dissertation, Arizona State University]. ProQuest Dissertations & Theses Global (9622997).

David, M. E. (2016). *A feminist manifesto for education.* Polity Press.

Dziech, B. & Weiner, L. (Eds.). (1990). *The lecherous professor: Sexual harassment on campus.* (2nd edition). University of Illinois Press.

Dziech, B. W. & Hawkins, M. W. (1998). *Sexual harassment in higher education: Reflections and new perspectives.* Garland Publishing.

Fisher, B., Daigle, L. & Cullen, F. (2010). *Unsafe in the ivory tower: The sexual victimization of college women.* SAGE.

Katz, M. & Vieland, V. (1993). *Get smart!: What you should know (but won't learn in class) about sexual harassment and sex discrimination* (2nd ed.). Feminist Press at the City University of New York.

Kipnis, L. (2017). *Unwanted advances: Sexual paranoia comes to campus.* Harper.

Lester, J. (2012). *Workplace bullying in higher education.* Routledge. https://ebook central.proquest.com/lib/ttu/detail.action?docID=1114638.

Lott, B. & Reilly, M. (1996). *Combating sexual harassment in higher education (Excellence in the academy).* National Education Association Professional Library.

Maylock, E. (2016). *Gender shrapnel in the academic workplace.* Palgrave Macmillan.

Paludi, M. A. (1990). *Ivory power sexual harassment on campus.* State University of New York Press.

Riggs, R., Murrell, P., Cutting, J. & United States Office of Educational Research Improvement. (1993). *Sexual harassment in higher education: From conflict to community (ASHE-ERIC higher education report, no. 2, 1993).* George Washington University, School of Education and Human Development.

Roiphe, K. (1993). *The morning after: Sex, fear, and feminism on campus.* Little, Brown and Co.

Spratlen, L. & University of Washington. (1988). *Prevention of sexual harassment in higher education: May 12–13, 1988, a regional workshop.* University of Washington.

Track Sexual Assault Investigations. (2017). [*The Chronicle of Higher Education's* Title IX investigation tracker project tracks federal investigations of colleges for possible violations of the gender-equity law Title IX involving alleged sexual violence]. https://projects.chronicle.com/titleix.

United States. Congress. House. Committee on Education Labor. Subcommittee on Higher Education, Lifelong Learning, Competitiveness. (2008). *Building on the success of 35 years of Title IX: Hearing before the Subcommittee on Higher Education, Lifelong Learning, and Competitiveness, Committee on Education and Labor, U.S. House of Representatives, One Hundred Tenth Congress, first session, hearing held in Washington, DC, June 19, 2007.* U.S. Government Publishing Office.

United States. Congress. Senate. Committee on Labor Human Resources. (1992). *University responses to racial and sexual harassment on campuses: Hearing before the Committee on Labor and Human Resources, United States Senate, One Hundred Second Congress, second session . . . September 10, 1992. (S. hrg.; 102–1152).* U.S. Government Publishing Office.

United States. Congress. House. Committee on Education the Workforce. Subcommittee on Higher Education Workforce Training, author. (2016). *Preventing and responding to sexual assault on college campuses: Hearing before the Subcommittee on Higher Education and Workforce Training, Committee on Education and the Workforce, House of Representatives, One Hundred Fourteenth Congress, first session, hearing held in Washington, DC, September 10, 2015.* U.S. Government Publishing Office.

References

Active Bystander Program & Mediation@MIT. (2004). Definition and philosophy. http://web.mit.edu/bystanders/definition/index.html.

Alexander, J. & Rhodes, J. (2011). Queer: An impossible subject for composition. *JAC: Journal of Advanced Composition, 31*(1–2), 177–206.

American Association of University Women. (2019). Know your rights at work: What should I do next. https://www.aauw.org/what-we-do/legal-resources/know -your-rights-at-work/workplace-sexual-harassment/employees-guide/.

Anahita, S. (2017). Trouble with Title IX. *Academe, 102*(3). https://www.aaup.org /article/trouble-title-ix#.XTiIG_17kbo.

Baker, C. N. (2007). *The women's movement against sexual harassment.* Cambridge University Press.

Bennett, J. (1991). How history changed Anita Hill. *New York Times.* https://www .nytimes.com/2019/06/17/us/anita-hill-women-power.html.

Bringing in the Bystander. (2019). https://cola.unh.edu/prevention-innovations -research-center/evidence-based.

Buzzanell, P. & Lucas, K. (2006). Gendered stories of career: Unfolding discourses of time, space, and identity. In B. Dow & J. Wood (Eds.). *The SAGE handbook of gender and communication.* (pp. 161–178). SAGE.

Campus Sexual Violence Elimination Act. S. 128 (2013). https://www.congress.gov /bill/113th-congress/senate-bill/128/text.

Cantor, D., Fisher, B., Chibnail, S., Townsend, R., Lee, H., Bruce, C. & Thomas, G. (2017). *Report on the AAU Campus Climate Survey on Sexual Assault and Sexual Misconduct.* https://www.aau.edu/sites/default/files/AAU-Files/Key-Issues/Cam pus-Safety/AAU-Campus-Climate-Survey-FINAL-10-20-17.pdf.

Carroll, J. (1992). Freshmen: Confronting sexual harassment in the classroom. *Composition Studies/Freshman English News, 20*(2), 60–73.

Condon, F. & Young, V. A. (Eds.). (2013). Anti-racist activism: Teaching rhetoric and writing [Special Issue]. *Across the Disciplines, 10.* https://wac.colostate.edu/atd /special/race/.

Conference on College Composition and Communication. (2016). Conference on College Composition and Communication standards for ethical conduct regard-ing sexual violence, sexual harassment, and hostile environments. http://cccc .ncte.org/cccc/resources/positions/ethical-conduct-sexual .

Conference on College Composition and Communication. (n.d.). Advocacy and activism. Retrieved May 21, 2019, from https://cccc.ncte.org/cccc/labor/advocacy.

Chief Elk, L. & Devereaux, S. (2014). The failure of bystander intervention. *The New Inquiry.* https://thenewinquiry.com/failure-of-bystander-intervention/.

Cushman, E. (2016). Translingual and decolonial approaches to meaning making. *College English, 78*(3), 234–242.

DeFour, D. (1990). The interface of racism and sexism on college Campuses. In M. Paludi (Ed.). *Ivory power* (pp. 45–52). State University of New York Press.

Daniel, B. (1994). Composing (as) power. *College Composition and Communication, 45*(2), 238–46.

Denning, S. (2011). How do you change an organizational culture? *Forbes.* https://www.forbes.com/sites/stevedenning/2011/07/23/how-do-you-change-an-organizational-culture/#7a3325c839dc.

Dolmage, J. (2017). *Academic ableism: Disability and higher education.* University of Michigan Press.

Dowd, M. (1991). The Thomas nomination: The senate and sexism; panel's handling of harassment allegation renews questions about an all-male club. *New York Times.* https://www.nytimes.com/1991/10/08/us/thomas-nomination-senate-sexism-panel-s-handling-harassment-allegation-renews.html .

Dziech, B. W. & Weiner, L. (1990). *The lecherous professor: Sexual harassment on campus* (2nd ed.). University of Illinois Press.

Edler, C. L. & Davila, B. (Eds.). (2019). *Defining, locating, and addressing bullying in the WPA workplace.* Utah State University Press.

Ellis, S. (2017). Analyzing sexual harassment in higher education. https://shanellis.github.io/2017/12/11/Harassment/.

Farley, L. (1978). *Sexual shakedown: The sexual harassment of women on the job.* McGraw-Hill.

Farley, L. (2017). I coined the term 'sexual harassment.' Corporations stole it. *New York Times.* https://www.nytimes.com/2017/10/18/opinion/sexual-harassment-corporations-steal.html.

Feldblum, C. & Lipnic, V. (2016). *Report of the co-chairs of the EEOC select task force on the study of harassment in the workplace.* https://www.eeoc.gov/eeoc/task_force/harassment/report.cfm.

Fenton, R. A., Mott, H. L., McCartan, K. & Rumney, P. N. S. (2016) *A review of evidence for bystander intervention to prevent sexual and domestic violence in universities.* Public Health England.

Ferganchick-Neufang, J. (1997). Harassment on-line. *Kairos: A Journal for Teachers of Writing in Webbed Environments, 2*(2). http://kairos.technorhetoric.net/2.2/coverweb/julia/honline.html.

Filipovitch, T. & McDearmon, M. (1998). The case of the harassed teacher. In C. M. Anson, L. K. Cafarelli, C. Rutz & M. R. Weis (Eds.), *Dilemmas in teaching: Cases for collaborative faculty reflection* (pp. 41–44). Mendota Press; The Collaborative for the Advancement of College Teaching & Learning.

Folz, C. (2016). No evidence that training prevents harassment, finds EEOC task force. https://www.shrm.org/hr-today/news/hr-news/pages/eeoc-harassment-task-force.asp.

Four-year institution survey. (2014). National Census of Writing. "What is your gender?" https://writingcensus.swarthmore.edu/survey/4?question_name=s4demo27&op=Submit#results.

Fredrickson, C. (2017). When will the 'Harvey Effect' reach academia? *The Atlantic.* https://www.theatlantic.com/education/archive/2017/10/when-will-the-harvey-effect-reach-academia/544388/.

Garrett, B. (2018). Hacking the curriculum, disabling composition pedagogy: The affordances of writing studio design. *Composition Forum, 39*. https://composi tionforum.com/issue/39/hacking.php.

Geiger, T.J. (2013). Unpredictable encounters: Religious discourse, sexuality, and the free exercise of rhetoric. *College English, 75*(3), 248–269.

Gluckman, N., Read, B., Mangan, K. & Quilantan, B. (2017). Sexual harassment and assault in higher ed: What's happened since Weinstein. *The Chronicle of Higher Education*. https://www.chronicle.com/article/Sexual-HarassmentAssault /241757.

Goldhill, O. & Slobin, S. (2017). One spreadsheet reveals the horrifying ubiquity of sexual harassment in academia. *Quartz*. https://qz.com/1153654/sexual-harass ment-in-academia-a-crowdsourced-survey-reveals-the-scale-metoo/.

Graber, M. (2018). A vindication of the rights of faculty. *Composition Studies, 46*(2).

Green Dot. (n.d.). Retrieved April 15, 2019, from https://alteristic.org/services/green -dot/ .

Harris, J. (2012). *A teaching subject: Composition since 1966*. Utah State University Press.

Harvey Weinstein timeline: How the scandal unfolded. (2019). *BBC News*. https:// www.bbc.com/news/entertainment-arts-41594672.

Henry, D. (1977, August 22). Yale faculty members charged with sexual harassment in suit. *New York Times* Archives. https://www.nytimes.com/1977/08/22/archives /yale-faculty-members-charged-with-sexual-harassment-in-suit.html.

Horner, B., Lu, M., Royster, J. J. & Trimbur, J. (2011). Language difference in writing: Toward a translingual approach. *College English, 73*(3), 303–321.

Horning, A. Contingent labor and the impact on teaching: Thoughts about the Indi-anapolis Resolution. *Literacy in Composition Studies, 4*(1), 73–76.

Inoue, A. B. (2015). *Antiracist writing assessment ecologies: Teaching and assessing writing for a socially just future*. The WAC Clearinghouse; Parlor Press. https:// wac.colostate.edu/books/perspectives/inoue.

Inoue, A. B. (2019). *Labor-based grading contracts: Building equity and inclusion in the compassionate writing classroom*. The WAC Clearinghouse; University Press of Colorado. https://wac.colostate.edu/books/perspectives/labor.

Inoue, A. B. & Poe, M. (Eds.). (2012). *Race and writing assessment*. Peter Lang.

Johnson, M. E. (2018). Only 1 in 4 women who have been sexually harassed tell their employers. Here's why they're afraid. *The Conversation*. http://theconversation .com/only-1-in-4-women-who-have-been-sexually-harassed-tell-their-employers -heres-why-theyre-afraid-97436.

Johnson, P., Widnall, S. & Benya, F. (Eds.). (2018). *Sexual harassment of women. Cli-mate, culture, and Consequences in academic sciences, engineering, and medicine*. https://doi.org/10.17226/24994.

Johnson, T. S. & Kerkhoff, S. (2018). #Metoo in English education. *English Educa-tion, 51*(1), 4–16.

Kahn, S., Lalicker, W. B. & Lynch-Biniek, A. (2017). *Contingency, exploitation, and soli-darity: Labor and action in English Composition*. The WAC Clearinghouse; Univer-sity Press of Colorado. https://wac.colostate.edu/books/perspectives/contingency.

Kairos. (n.d.). Slivae Rhetorica. Retrieved February 22, 2019, from http://rhetoric
.byu.edu/.

Kantor, J. & Twohey, M. (2017). Harvey Weinstein paid off sexual harassment accusers for decades. *New York Times.* https://www.nytimes.com/2017/10/05/us
/harvey-weinstein-harassment-allegations.html.

Kelsky, K. (2017). Sexual harassment in the academy: A crowdsourced survey.
https://theprofessorisin.com/2017/12/01/a-crowdsourced-survey-of-sexual
-harassment-in-the-academy/.

Lamos, S. (2008). Language, literacy, and the institutional dynamics of racism:
Late–1960s writing instruction for "High-Risk" African American undergraduate
students at one predominantly white university. *College Composition and Communication, 60*(1), 46–81.

Lewis, N. (1991, October 7). Law professor accuses Thomas of sexual harassment in
the 1980s. *New York Times.* https://www.nytimes.com/1991/10/07/us/law
-professor-accuses-thomas-of-sexual-harassment-in-1980-s.html.

MacKinnon, C. (1979). *Sexual harassment of working women.* Yale University
Press.

Maimon, E. P. (2018). *Leading academic change: Vision, strategy, and transformation.*
Stylus Publishing.

Mayock, E. (2016). *Gender shrapnel in the academic workplace.* Palgrave Macmillan.

Mazza, E. (2017.) Obama: Elect more women "because men seem to be having some
problems these days." *Huffpost.* https://www.huffpost.com/entry/barack-obama
-women_n_5a24dd9ce4b03350e0b7a354 .

McLaughlin. H., Uggen, C. & Blackstone, A. (2012). Sexual harassment, workplace authority, and the paradox of power. *American Sociological Review, 77*(4).
625–647.

Micche, L. R. (2018) From the editor. *Composition Studies, 46*(2),10–11.

Miller, C. C. (2017, April 10). It's not just Fox: Why women don't report sexual harassment. *New York Times.* https://www.nytimes.com/2017/04/10/upshot/its-not
-just-fox-why-women-dont-report-sexual-harassment.html.

Nemy, E. (1975, August 19). Women begin to speak out against sexual harassment at
work. *New York Times* Archives. https://www.nytimes.com/1975/08/19/archives
/women-begin-to-speak-out-against-sexual-harassment-at-work.html.

Passwater, T. (2019). Precarious spaces, institutional places. *Composition Forum, 41.*
https://compositionforum.com/issue/41/precarious-spaces.php.

Penrose, A. (2012). Professional identity in a contingent-labor profession: Expertise,
autonomy, community in composition teaching. *WPA: Writing Program Administration, 35*(2), 108–126. https://csal.colostate.edu/docs/cwpa/syllabus/Profes
sional-Identity-Contingent-Labor.pdf.

Perryman-Clark, S. M. (2016). Who we are(n't) assessing: Racializing language and
writing assessment in Writing Program Administration. *College English, 79*(2),
206–211.

Poe, M., Inoue, A. B. & Elliot, N. (2018). *Writing assessment, social justice, and the
advancement of opportunity.* The WAC Clearinghouse; University Press of Colorado. https://wac.colostate.edu/books/perspectives/assessment.

Quina, K. (1990). The victimizations of women. In M. Paludi (Ed.). *Ivory power*. (pp. 93–102). State University of New York Press.

Rabinowitz, V. (1990). Coping with sexual harassment. In M. Paludi (Ed.), *Ivory power*. (pp. 103–118). State University of New York Press.

Roehling M. V. & Huang, J. (2018). Sexual harassment training effectiveness: An interdisciplinary review and call for research. *Journal of Organizational Behavior*, 39, 134–150.

Royster, J. J. (2000). *Traces in the stream: Literacy and social change among African American women*. University of Pittsburgh Press.

Sandberg, S. (2017). *The 1992 presidential race was once summed up . . .* [Facebook post]. https://www.facebook.com/sheryl/posts/10159569315265177?utm_source =newsletter&utm_medium=email&utm_campaign=newsletter_axiosam&stream =top-stories.

Sanders, B. (1990). Forewords: An ecological perspective. In M. Paludi (Ed.) *Ivory power. Sexual harassment on campus* (pp. xvi-xvii). State University of New York Press.

Schell, E. & Stock, P. L. (Eds.). (2001). *Moving a mountain: Transforming the role of contingent faculty in composition studies and higher education*. National Council of Teachers of English.

Scott, T. (2009). *Dangerous writing: Understanding the political economy of composition*. Utah State University Press.

The University of Texas at Austin School of Social Work Institute on Domestic Violence & Sexual Assault. (2017). Cultivating learning and safe environments. An empirical study of prevalence and perceptions of sexual harassment, stalking, dating/domestic abuse and violence, and unwanted sexual contact. https://www .utsystem.edu/sites/default/files/sites/clase/files/.../ut-austin-.

Two-year institution survey. (2014). National Census of Writing. What is your gender? https://writingcensus.swarthmore.edu/survey/2?question_name=s2q313& othercohorts=&op=Submit#results.

U. S. Equal Opportunity Employment. (n.d.). Facts about sexual harassment. Retrieved December 4, 2018, from https://www.eeoc.gov/eeoc/publications/fs-sex .cfm.

U.S. Equal Employment Opportunity Commission. (1990). Notice number N–915-050. https://www.eeoc.gov/policy/docs/currentissues.html.

U.S. Equal Employment Opportunity Commission. (n.d.). *Sex-based discrimination*. Retrieved December 4, 2018 from https://www.eeoc.gov/laws/types/sex.cfm.

Villanueva, V. (2006). Blind: Talking about the new racism. *Writing Center Journal*, 26(1), 3–19.

Vrotsos, L. W. (2018). School of Public Health admins flag classes for review after students report "insults." *The Crimson*. https://www.thecrimson.com/article/2018 /4/5/hsph-insults-classes-flagged/.

Weaver, M. (2004). Censoring what tutors' clothing "says": First Amendment rights/ writes within tutorial space. *Writing Center Journal*, 24(2), 19–36.

Welch, N. & Scott, T. (Eds.) (2016). *Composition in the age of austerity*. Utah State University Press.

White, E. C. (1987). *Kaironomia: On the will-to-invent.* Cornell University Press.

Wood, T., Dolmage, J., Price, M. & Lewiecki-Wilson, C. (2014). [Where we are] Moving beyond disability 2.0 in composition studies. *Composition Studies, 42*(2), 147–150.

Zilman, C. (2017). Barack Obama and Sheryl Sandberg say power is an antidote to harassment. It's not so simple. *Fortune.* http://fortune.com/2017/12/11/barack -obama-sheryl-sandberg-sexual-harassment-women-power/ .

Contributors

Aaron Barlow teaches English at New York City College of Technology of the City University of New York. His books include *The Rise of the Blogosphere* and *The Cult of Individualism*. He is former Faculty Editor of *Academe*. His primary focus is the teaching of first-year composition.

Darsie Bowden is Professor Emerita at DePaul University where she ran the First-Year Writing program. She served on the executive board of the Council of Writing Program Administration and is the author of *The Mythology of Voice*. Her articles have been published in the *Journal of Writing Assessment, WPA Journal, Composition Studies,* and the *Journal of College Composition and Communication.*

Kefaya Diab is a post-doctoral fellow at Indiana University. She engages rhetorical theory and cultural (digital) rhetorics in theorizing activist movements in the Arab world and adopts a critical pedagogy that invites students to utilize digital rhetorics and composition as tools to promote social justice. Her work has appeared in *Composition Studies* and *Paideia–16 Textbook.*

William Duffy is Associate Professor and Coordinator of the Writing, Rhetoric, and Technical Communication program at the University of Memphis, where he teaches courses in composition, rhetoric, and professional writing. His book *Beyond Conversation: Collaboration and the Production of Writing* is forthcoming from Utah State University Press.

Patricia Freitag Ericsson is Associate Professor Emeritus at Washington State University, where she served as Director of Composition and Director of the Digital Technology and Culture Degree Program. She has published widely in journals, including *Journal of Teaching Writing, English Education, The Clearing House,* and *Computers and Composition,* as well as edited collections. She co-edited *Machine Scoring of Student Essays: Truth and Consequences* with Rich Haswell.

Ti Macklin is a lecturer at Boise State University, where she teaches undergraduate and graduate courses in composition and rhetoric. She has published in *Composition Forum, Journal of Response to Writing, California English,* and a number of edited collections. She is Associate Editor of the *Journal of Writing Assessment* and Editor of the *JWA Reading List.*

Craig A. Meyer is Assistant Professor of English at Texas A&M University Kingsville, where he specializes in rhetoric, academic writing, and creative writing. His research focuses on histories of rhetoric, social justice, distinctions between global ethos and local ethos, disability studies, and rhetoric of popular culture including Star Trek. He has published in *CCCC-IP, Humanities,* and *Writing Spaces.*

Whitney Myers is Associate Professor of English at Texas Wesleyan University, where she teaches first-year writing and upper-level writing classes as well as themed courses such as The Rhetoric of Popular Culture. Her most recent publications focus on rhetorical histories in off-reservation boarding schools, yoga, and feminism.

Mark Shealy is Instructor at Tennessee Technical University, where he teaches first-year writing. He is also Adjunct Assistant Professor at the University of Maryland Global Campus, where he teaches advanced technical communication. He has published in *Rhetoric Society Quarterly (RSQ)*, *Sweetland Digital Rhetoric Collaborative*, and *Enculturation: A Journal of Rhetoric, Writing, and Culture*.

Dianna Winslow is Assistant Director and Writing Instruction Specialist for the Center for Teaching, Learning, and Technology at California Polytechnic, San Luis Obispo. She works with faculty on writing instruction in general education and discipline-specific contexts and coaches faculty on scholarly writing and writing for professional advancement.

Kathleen Blake Yancey is Kellogg Hunt Professor and Distinguished Research Professor at Florida State University. Author/editor of 16 books, she has published over 100 articles and book chapters. She is the recipient of several awards, including the Donald Murray Prize, the FSU Graduate Teaching Award (twice), the CCCC Exemplar Award, and NCTE's Squire Award.